THE VENTURE FUND BLUEPRINT

How to Access Capital, Achieve Launch, and Actualize Growth

by Shea Tate-Di Donna and Kaego Ogbechie Rust

HOUNDSTOOTH
PRESS

The Venture Fund Blueprint
How to Access Capital, Achieve Launch, and Actualize Growth

ISBN 978-1-5445-3595-1 Hardcover
ISBN 978-1-5445-3596-8 Paperback
ISBN 978-1-5445-3597-5 Ebook

First edition 2022

by Shea Tate-Di Donna and Kaego Ogbechie Rust

All individuals and fund names were used with their approval.

Dedication

It is only with a diversity of intellect that we can create
a variety of solutions and build our best future.
We dedicate this work to those who dare to change
the face of venture, finance, and investing.

Acknowledgments

Sincerest appreciation to the following individuals
for their invaluable contributions:

Julie Castro Abrams, How Women Invest
Raanan Bar-Cohen, Resolute Ventures
Phil Black, True Ventures
David Brown, Techstars
John Burke, PROOF and Angel Investor
Calixte Davis, Calixte Davis Design
Josh Felser, Climactic
John Gannon, GoingVC
Michael Gibson, 1517 Fund
Jennifer Gill Roberts, Grit Ventures
Tracy Gray, The 22 Fund
Kirsten Green, Forerunner Ventures
Charles Hudson, Precursor Ventures
Jim Jensen, Wilson Sonsini Goodrich & Rosati
Eric Krichevsky, RYLNYC
Scott Kupor, Andreessen Horowitz
Frances Luu, Storm Ventures
Patrick Mahoney, RW Ventures and Angel Investor
Julie Mauser, LifeSci Venture Partners
Matt McInerney, Township
Harsh Patel, Wireframe Ventures
Alison Rosenthal, Leadout Capital
Jason Rowley, Capbase
Roberto Sanabria, Expa
Michael Seibel, Y Combinator
Danielle Strachman, 1517 Fund
Adam Tope, DLA Piper
Eric Woo, Revere
Lan Xuezhao, Basis Set Ventures
Alan Yang, Towne Advisory Services
Elizabeth Yin, Hustle Fund
Timothy Young, Dropbox

Table of Contents

Introduction

Introduction

We are lifelong learners, always striving to be our better selves and constantly pushing ahead to reach new heights. Naturally, when we set out to learn something new, we do the research, and we also talk to smart people. People who are of the highest caliber, are eager to share their finest techniques and best practices, and want us to benefit from their extensive experiences in order to optimize our collective resources.

We wrote this book for aspiring fund managers to in fact succeed. To win. To share with you our 10,000 hours of application, our best practices, and our lessons learned from people we respect.

During the past few years, we have had over 3,000 conversations with more than 400 fund managers. Our careers took us through True Ventures and Goldman Sachs in venture capital, early-stage ecosystems, the private and public markets, and finance. Curiously, the same important questions kept arising time and time again: "How do I launch my fund?" "What do I need to get started?" and "Where can I find an example from another fund?"

As we dug deeper, we realized that, when creating their own funds, fund managers simply desired access to exclusive information in order to save time, save money, and free themselves to do what they do best: find stellar deals.

Our book brings together tactical examples in a guidebook format for you to begin the journey of establishing your fund. It is intended to be a blueprint that is coffee-stained, dog-eared, and marked up in the margins by your desk. The real-world examples we provide in this book serve as step-by-step instructions, tips and tricks, and shared materials to use in real time.

We wrote this book for the next generation of newly minted venture capitalists with a diversity of intellects. Regardless of your starting point — whether you are a lifetime angel investor, venture apprentice, or seasoned startup operator — this book will assist you in smoothly navigating your fund launch.

We will usher you from idea to vision and strategy, then all the way to your first investment and much more. You will learn to launch and maintain a fund and gain insights on operations, fundraising, legal, and new-fund formation.

What comes next is a simple guidebook. We have organized this content into ten chapters:

1. *Investment Thesis:* Identifying your key differentiators and investment strategy
2. *Fund Preparation:* Creating an outline of timing and costs ahead of fundraising
3. *Fundraising:* Planning and prioritizing the timeline of your fundraise
4. *Limited Partner Program:* Corresponding with your investors and fiduciaries

5. *Portfolio Management:* Cultivating your portfolio companies to maximize growth
6. *Operations:* Selecting providers across your business and organizational planning
7. *Fund Administration & Accounting:* Assessing financial and accounting elements of your fund
8. *Portfolio Composition*: Reviewing common portfolio constructions
9. *Legal:* Starting your fund formation and deal documentation
10. *Longevity & Growth:* Positioning your fund for the future to build a long-lasting firm

At the end of every chapter, you will find appendices containing supplemental examples to bring you one step closer to your fund goals. You will have the necessary insight to smoothly launch and grow your firm. Do not stop there. Come back to this book when you need a refresher or after you have achieved your first fund launch and start delving into your second, third, or fourth funds and beyond. One step at a time, you will develop resilience to persevere through the hard parts and endeavor to create something that will endure.

Our best,
Shea Tate-Di Donna & Kaego Ogbechie Rust

Scan this QR code

or visit

https://www.venturefundblueprint.com

to see the interactive workbook and learn more about
The Venture Fund Blueprint

Chapter 1
Investment Thesis

Chapter 1
Investment Thesis

Designing Your Strategic Vision

You should begin your endeavor with both a vision and a strategy. Your vision is your desired outcome, and your strategy is the collection of resources used to reach the desired outcome. Vision and strategy share an iterative and codependent relationship: the more you clarify your intended outcome, the more apparent your resources become. By continually refining your vision and strategy, you greatly increase your likelihood of success along your journey toward launching a fund.

Every fund manager has the same "macro" vision and the same "macro" strategy: — to operate a successful fund and raise capital from investors to invest in portfolio companies that generate a multiple return on investment. Given these broad, expected consistencies across fund managers, you must find a way to distinguish yourself from the pack. Your vision and strategy are critical components of establishing your fund's differentiator and investment thesis. An investment thesis is an overall set of principles that you will use for your fund to make investment decisions. Your investment thesis should give your investors a better sense of your philosophy for investing and expected portfolio composition, while also revealing what gives you a competitive advantage that other funds do not have.

After you have asked yourself the key questions outlined in this chapter, you should be able to describe the three core components of your investment thesis, including (1) what you invest in, (2) what your competitive advantage is to understand, access, or own those investments, and (3) how this advantage benefits your performance and leads to returns.

New Fund Manager Questions

The following series of questions will help you clearly define your vision and strategy as a new fund manager. Each question will help form your investment thesis, which is the set of principles that you will use to make investment decisions.

Step #1
Goal: Set Your Vision

- What is your fund's specific focus? Are you targeting a specific region, market, sector, stage, or business type? Will you focus on investing in industry-changing companies, or companies focusing on fintech, insurtech, real estate tech, agtech, edtech?
- What role will your fund play in the space in which it operates? Will your fund aim to disrupt an existing industry or bridge a market gap?
- What do you want your fund and firm to be known for in the market? What are the guiding principles that your fund offers to investments, such as technical expertise, quick turnaround times to invest, support, availability, diversity of intellect, coaching, or connecting portfolio companies to partnerships/recruiting/investors?
- What fund or firm do you most respect?
- What are the goals of your investors? What quantifiable return on invested capital will you obtain for investors over the fund's lifetime of approximately ten years? Will your investors aim for access to co-investments or access to direct portfolio company investments?

- What does success look like for you in two years? In five years? In ten years?
- If you have made prior investments and plan to make similar investments, answer the following three questions for each:
  - How did you source that investment?
  - Why did you invest?
  - Once you invested, how did you add value?

Step #2
Goal: Define Your Strategy

- Background
  - What are your strengths and interests as an investor? Are you process-focused; an expert in your field; or known for high-level support, quick turnaround times, availability, coaching, or connecting portfolio companies to partnerships/recruiting/investors?
  - If you do not have a "traditional" venture background, what is your alternative illustration of investment ability and long-term track record, such as a foundry fund, advising, angel investing, or Founder networks? What is your related investing track record? Have you successfully made related investments or seen great returns? What is your prior experience?
  - Do you have permission to disclose your prior track record to potential fund investors and the ability to update said track record in the future? Do you have access to track record data and the ability to have a reference confirm such data?
  - What experience can you draw from to inform your investment decisions?

- What special insights have you gained from your experiences? Have you identified a gap in the market, an untapped region, or an opportunity for an improved process?
- What are your team dynamics? How do those dynamics help you to work as a functional and efficient unit? How long have you known each other, how well do you know each other, have you invested together, and how do you make decisions?
- Do you have any reservations or doubts about launching a fund? Are there any reasons that you should not do this?
- Competition
  - Who would be your fund's competitors, and what differentiates your fund from them, such as brand, reputation, personal relationship, and expertise? Who might receive investor capital instead of you?
  - Are there specific funds that came before you, on which you would model your approach? Who do you see as the market leaders on performance, brand, team, and relationships with portfolio companies?
  - Why does another fund like yours need to exist? What metrics demonstrate that your advantage is appealing?
- Outlook
  - What macro challenges do you believe portfolio companies face in the market, and why would your firm be best positioned to assist? What are some pressing issues portfolio companies need your help with, such as challenges recruiting locally, challenges with operational support, or challenges accessing capital?

- How long do you expect to raise your fund? Note that it often takes a first-time fund manager 12 to 18 months[1] or longer to raise an initial fund, while the majority of fund managers never go on to raise a second fund at all.
- What impediments, roadblocks, or obstacles do you foresee in the first three years, such as a lack of salary while fundraising, a smaller first fund than anticipated, or overwhelming contribution of personal net worth into your fund?
- How will you pay for expenses incurred prior to raising your fund? How will you make payment if your fund does not get raised?

- Investor Base
  - How many investors do you intend to target based on the average minimum check size expected?
  - Who are your target investors, and what are their relative advantages and disadvantages, including high net worth individuals, family offices, fund-of-funds, endowments, foundations, universities, public or private pension plans, insurance and financial services companies, investment partnerships, governments and/or sovereign wealth funds, strategic corporate investors, consultants who act as gatekeepers, or other institutions?
  - How will you gain access to those investors? How will you leverage your existing relationships and your network to raise your fund? Will you work with "placement agents" that charge you a fee based on the percentage of new money raised and may help find interested investors?

- What is your expected diligence process on investors, and what is their expected diligence process on you and your firm, which is the act of evaluating potential risks and fit?
- Will you have an anchor investor? If so, will the anchor investor receive preferred terms such as a reduced management fee, reduced carried interest, or preferential co-investment terms?
- How many investors do you intend to target? What is your expected close rate or percentage?
- What is the minimum investment amount for investors based on the minimum amount of capital needed to make the fund viable?
- What will motivate your investors to invest in your fund and close in a timely manner, such as returns projections based on your previous returns or track record, capital preservation, diversification, industry knowledge, or ownership opportunities?
- Do your prospective investors' expectations match your investment thesis? Note that high net worth individuals may have more condensed timelines than institutional investors.
- What challenges might your potential investors face? Will your potential investors require a certain level of communication and transparency with you?
- Portfolio Companies
  - Which sector(s) will you invest in, such as AI, SaaS, life sciences, fintech, security, retail, or hardware? Will you invest in multiple industries? Will you be industry agnostic?

- Which business models will you invest in, such as B2B (business-to-business), B2C (business-to-consumer), or B2B2C (business-to-business-to-consumer)?
- In which stage will you target investing? For example, there are several stages of investing that represent the funding a company may receive, generally including:
  - "Pre-seed" stage, when a company is first getting off the ground with less than $1 million raised;
  - "Seed" stage when the first official convertible note or equity stake is offered to investors, with approximately $1 million to $4 million raised;
  - "Series A" stage, when a company typically receives its first priced round from investors, with approximately $4 million to $10 million raised;
  - "Series B to Series D" stages, with approximately $10 million to $100 million-plus raised, and
  - "Late-stage/growth," when a company is often rapidly expanding, with approximately multi millions raised.
- What is your due diligence process to review companies before deciding to invest?
- How much time will you spend with a company before deciding to invest? Will you require spending a minimum amount of time, weekly or monthly, with the company first?
- What additional support or value-add can you provide portfolio companies beyond capital? Will you offer recruiting, advising, coaching, public relations, strategic partnerships, or co-investors for the current round?

- What is your target ownership percentage of each portfolio company, if any?
- How many Board/observer seats will you occupy for each portfolio company? Are there circumstances where you will not take a Board seat?
- Why would a company choose to take capital from your fund over a competitive fund? Why would a company prefer your brand, reputation, personal relationship, expertise, terms, speed of execution, or governance?
- What do you want your portfolio makeup to look like by the end of your fund's investment period? What are your goals for the type of companies, number of companies, overall ownership, regional exposure, and diversity of your portfolio?
- Will you "follow-on" by committing capital to a portfolio company's future rounds? How much will you initially invest in each portfolio company, or will there be a range? How much will you reserve for follow-on rounds, and what is the expected timing? What do you want your portfolio makeup to look like by the end of the fund's investment period?

Step #3
Goal: Build Your Fund Elements

- Viability
  - How will you structure your funds? Will you be the solo fund manager or will there be other senior investment professionals? Will your investment team have similar or varying investment philosophies and/or cover different sectors?

- How will you structure your investment team? Do you have a formal investment committee or Board of advisors? What is their role?
- Will you have individuals assist with deal flow or due diligence? Will you have scouts, analysts, associates, principals, or venture partners?
- How will you scale your investment team? How will you add additional investment professionals and/or partners without significantly increasing costs?
- How do you intend to scale your fund's investments? Will you alter the amount of your initial check size, adjust the amount of follow-on investments in the future, or tranche your investment based on achieving milestones?
- What is the amount of capital that may be paid to your fund's partners as compensation annually?
- What is the minimum amount of capital that you need to raise for your fund model to work over its lifetime?

- Considerations
  - Will you have outside time commitments while managing your fund, such as non-investment Board seats, a role at a company, advisory positions to companies, or an entrepreneur-in-residence role?

- Understanding the Market
  - Have you spoken with numerous fund managers before getting started in order to understand the day-to-day commitment, advice, and tips for being a fund manager?
  - Have you spoken with peers, advisors, and industry participants to understand general costs associated with raising a

fund? Have you spoken to advisors? Have you spoken to lawyers who will head your legal team and fund formation, fund administrators who will lead the financial setup of your fund, and banks that will hold your capital?

Starting a fund can be a daunting yet rewarding endeavor for a fund manager. Begin with a vision and strategy to help build your investment thesis and ensure you can clearly speak to your differentiators as a fund manager, while staying organized to hit the right milestones along the way.

Scan this QR code

or visit
https://www.venturefundblueprint.com/blueprints/investmentthesis

to see the interactive workbook and learn more about
The Venture Fund Blueprint

Appendix

1.1 Example: Investment Thesis — 1517 Fund[2]

Review the following investment thesis example and, later, use the exercises in this chapter to help build your own investment thesis.

1517 Fund invests in brilliant young Founders without a college degree by offering a $250k check and mentorship when they are going into pilots, which results in the startups finding product-market fit before their seed round and in us becoming the first phone call of any young person starting a company and makes for great economics as the first institutional investor in the deal.

Appendix

1.2 Example: Investment Thesis — Grit Ventures[3]

Review the following investment thesis example and, later, use the exercises in this chapter to help build your own investment thesis.

Grit Ventures invests in early-stage AI and robotics startups, providing go-to-market expertise to significantly de-risk early-stage hardware investing, which results in a conviction portfolio of Robotics as a Service companies that are able to scale more quickly for less capital.

Appendix

1.3 Example: Investment Thesis — Resolute Ventures[4]

Review the following investment thesis example and, later, use the exercises in this chapter to help build your own investment thesis.

Resolute Ventures invests in Founders at the very beginning of their journey. We are not category- or sector-specific and tend to focus our due diligence on getting to really know the founding team by investing in what today would be considered the angel round but with a full seed check. We are able to lead our investments and partner with Founders as early as possible, which results in us being aligned with our Founders as they scale up their companies.

Appendix

1.4 Example: Investment Thesis — Sequoia Capital[5]

Review the following investment thesis example and, later, use the exercises in this chapter to help build your own investment thesis.

We help the daring build legendary companies, from idea to IPO and beyond. Our advantage comes from four decades of legendary Founders helping each other. Our team mirrors the Founders with whom we partner: hungry overachievers with a deep-rooted need to win. Many come from humble backgrounds. Many are immigrants. Many formed or built companies of their own before joining Sequoia. Each shares the mindset of an entrepreneur and knows what it means to walk that path. While we're sometimes called investors, that is not our frame of mind. We consider ourselves partners for the long term.

Appendix

1.5 Example: Investment Thesis — Y Combinator[6]

Review the following investment thesis example and, later, use the exercises in this chapter to help build your own investment thesis.

Y Combinator (YC) developed a new model of startup funding. Twice a year, we invest a small amount of money in a large number of startups (approximately 200). The YC partners work closely with each company to get them into the best possible shape and refine their pitch to investors. Each cycle culminates in Demo Day, when the startups present their business plans to a carefully selected audience of investors. Demo Day is a unique setting where companies are able to participate in a startup bootcamp, meet their potential investors, and connect with future customers. YC focuses on putting leverage back on the Founder side, and approximately 30% of YC's teams go on to raise a Series A. We don't target specific types of companies for Y Combinator, and we don't break out our companies into different groups by industry. We help all of our startups make things people want.

Appendix

1.6 Exercise: Investment Thesis

Use the template below to create your own investment thesis. This will help you outline the differentiator that gives you a competitive advantage that other funds do not have.

We invest in <u><type of founder or company></u>, by doing <u><your competitive advantage: how you understand, access, own more of them></u>, which results in <u><benefit to performance></u>.

Appendix

1.7 Exercise: Story

Use the outline below to create your own story and narrative.

With the <u>\<market opportunity / gap in the market / region untapped\></u> experience, <u>\<firm name\></u>'s expertise in <u>\<team advantages\></u> generates <u>\<benefit\></u>. Investing in <u>\<type of Founder or company\></u> by doing \<competitive advantage / business model\> results in <u>\<benefit to performance\></u>. Based on our track record of <u>\<number of funds to date and past metrics such as TVPI/ DPI/IRR/returns\></u>, <u>\<firm name\></u> solves <u>\<problem for industry, portfolio companies and/or investors\></u>, and the success of the investments will return <u>\<portfolio company growth and goals for the investors and portfolio companies\></u>. \<Firm name\> is raising <u>\<$$\></u> and has received <u>\<$$\></u> in commitment from <u>\<anchor limited partner\></u>. <u>\<Additional limited partner investor(s)\></u> have also secured endorsements and increased investment amount commitments. The target first close is <u>\<date or quarter\></u>.

Appendix

1.8 Exercise: Investor Profile

Use the template below to create an investor profile of who will invest in your fund.

<Firm name> is seeking funding from <type of LP: family office, high net worth individual, fund of funds, institutions, hedge funds, pension funds>. The anchor LP is <investor name> with <preferential terms> With <$$ min capital> needed, <firm name> is seeking <#> Limited Partners with a minimum check size of <$$>. Limited Partners want to invest in <firm name> because of <performance: ROI, capital preservation, diversification, industry knowledge, ownership opportunities>. Limited Partners with the <expectation/timeline> are more suitable to invest in <firm name>.

Appendix

1.9 Exercise: Structure

Use the outline below to build an overview of the structure of your fund.

<Firm name>

Comprises of <# GPs: single, multiple> in <# venture partners, investment committees, associates>. To scale the investments <follow-on amount, check size, pro-rata amounts> will be attuned along with the <added team members: GPs, associates, venture partners> to increase network without increasing costs. The portfolio will consist of <# portfolio companies> with <# of new investments> per year with an average check size of <$$> and <$$> allotted for follow-ons. In order to prove the fund's investment thesis, <$$> is the minimum needed with <#>% to pay for General Partner salaries.

Appendix

1.10 Exercise: External Commitments

Use the table below to highlight whether you will have outside time commitments while managing your fund.

Item	Detail
Boards	<#>
At current company	<Role>
Companies advising	<#>
Entrepreneur-in-residence	<Role>

Appendix

Appendix 1.10 Exercise: External Commitments *(continued)*

List your formal investment committees or advisors, if any, and their role.

Advisor/Committee	Role *(investment quality, due diligence, etc.)*
<Name>	<Role>
<Name>	<Role>
<Name>	<Role>
<Name>	<Role>

Appendix

1.11 Exercise: Understanding the Market

Use the table below to track when you have spoken with fund managers, advisors, peers, or industry contacts such as venture banks, lawyers, or fund administrators, etc. Apply those conversations to understanding the day-to-day work, costs, and tips around running your fund.

Item	Fund Managers and Peers	Referral	Date	Notes
1	<Fund managers, advisors, peers, banks, lawyers, etc.>	<Referral>	<Date>	<Notes>
2	<Fund managers, advisors, peers, banks, lawyers, etc.>	<Referral>	<Date>	<Notes>
3	<Fund managers, advisors, peers, banks, lawyers, etc.>	<Referral>	<Date>	<Notes>
4	<Fund managers, advisors, peers, banks, lawyers, etc.>	<Referral>	<Date>	<Notes>
5	<Fund managers, advisors, peers, banks, lawyers, etc.>	<Referral>	<Date>	<Notes>
6	<Fund managers, advisors, peers, banks, lawyers, etc.>	<Referral>	<Date>	<Notes>
7	<Fund managers, advisors, peers, banks, lawyers, etc.>	<Referral>	<Date>	<Notes>

NOTES

Chapter 2
Fund Preparation

Chapter 2
Fund Preparation

Laying the Groundwork

In order to pitch your fund to prospective investors, you need to first understand the terrain of the existing marketplace. Ahead of fundraising and launching your fund, you must understand the operational and capital hurdles you will inevitably face, the costs, and the commitment. Based on this understanding, you can successfully define how your fund will fit into the existing market, what differentiates your fund from others in your space, and how to become ready to deploy the investment thesis you established in the previous chapter. With the number of new venture funds growing 245% over the past ten years,[7] with 415 in 2010 and crossing 1,000 in 2020, this is now more important than ever.

By making a clear plan in advance to identify your fund's costs, personal capital, time allocation, deal sourcing, portfolio composition, and philosophy, you will demonstrate readiness and maturity to your prospective investors and improve your chances of articulating why they should invest in your fund.

Pre-Fundraise Action Plan

Although your fund may evolve over time, your initial success may depend on how you first enter the market. Outlined below is an action plan to help you establish the basic elements of your fund before you prepare to launch your fundraising effort.

Step #1

Goal: Outline Investment Thesis and Story

- Complete New Fund Manager Questions to outline your vision and strategy (see Investment Thesis chapter)
- Sketch out your investment thesis

Step #2

Goal: Understand Fund Managers' Day-to-Day

- Speak with ten or more fund managers and peers to begin to understand the day-to-day operations of a fund and ask for advice and tips on launching a fund

---

Step #3

Goal: Understand Fund Costs

- Speak with ten or more industry participants such as fund managers, law firms, fund administrators, banking providers, tax advisors, accountants, and peers to understand general costs associated with raising and managing a fund
- Consider common costs around fundraising:
  - Legal and tax consulting

- ○ Organizational costs
- ○ Travel expenses
- ○ Placement agent fees, if you use an agent to help you find interested investors
- Consider common costs around managing a fund:
  - ○ Fund-level costs:
    - General partner (GP) commitment
    - Management fees
    - Deal-related expenses
    - Fund administration
    - Legal, accounting, and tax consulting
  - ○ Management company costs:
    - Manager and employee salaries
    - Office space
    - Travel, if not reimbursed by the fund

Step #4

Goal: Evaluate Time Commitment

- Evaluate the time you will spend on the following activities, both during and after the fund is raised, to better understand your potential schedule:
  - ○ Fundraising
  - ○ Marketing, which may include speaking engagements, industry events, networking
  - ○ Deal sourcing and due diligence
  - ○ Investor communication
  - ○ Portfolio company monitoring, check-ins, and Board management

- Firm management, operations, and vendor management
- Hiring
- Take inventory of your other time commitments:
  - Estimate your current time commitments on a weekly, monthly, quarterly basis
- Evaluate the impact of your other time commitments:
  - What can you off-load from your schedule?
  - What are your continuing commitments? Do you have ongoing Board roles, coaching commitments, or advising or consulting roles to fulfill?

Step #5

Goal: Determine Investment Focus

- Is your investment model generalist, thematic, thesis-driven, or sector-focused?
  - Why?

Step #6

Goal: Set Return Goals

- What does success look like over a ten-year horizon?
  - Home-run strategy
  - Hits business
  - 3x return (or more) on invested capital

Step #7

Goal: Model Your Fund

- Determine fund structure:
  - Ideal number of portfolio companies

- ○ Average check size
- ○ Number of new investments per year
- ○ Sector
- ○ Stage
- ○ Amount of initial and follow-on investments

Step #8

Goal: Define Internal Team Structure and Specific Roles

- Managers, principals, investment professionals:
  - ○ What is the growth strategy? Will you add more general partners? Will another partner take over from you? Will the firm cease to exist once you are gone?
  - ○ Will you raise multiple funds over ten years?
  - ○ What are specific roles for sourcing and monitoring deals?
  - ○ Will you consider a scout program to have individuals help deal source and bring promising deals to your fund?
- Operations:
  - ○ What functions will be handled internally?
  - ○ What functions will be outsourced?
- Location of office(s)

Step #9

Goal: Develop a Capital Deployment Strategy for Investments

- What is needed before allocating capital to an investment?
  - ○ Revenue, traction, and/or growth requirements
  - ○ Minimum, average, and max check size

- What qualifications must an entrepreneur meet to receive your investment?
- How much time must you spend with an entrepreneur before you invest?
- What is your background and reference check process for entrepreneurs?

- What is your due diligence process for prospective investments?
  - Revenue, customer lists, business plan, financials, burn, projections, hiring and marketing plan
- How long do you plan to deploy initial capital?
  - Take into consideration that the investment period is typically five years, the average life of a fund is ten years, and many early-stage firms deploy capital more quickly
- How will fundraising overlap with deployment?
  - If well planned, the fundraising of your second fund will overlap with deployment so that you do not run out of initial investable capital in the first fund before the new fund is raised; otherwise, you may be forced to forgo a desirable investment

Step #10

Goal: Create a Process for Sourcing Deal Flow

- Where will your deal flow, or the stream of companies and potential investments for your fund, come from now versus in the future?
  - Inbound calls
  - Events

- ○ Content created
- ○ Accelerators
- ○ Communities

Note: Many funds receive deal flow from similar credible channels, such as YC, Techstars, StartX, and others

Step #11

Goal: Refine Your Investment Philosophy

- Deal position — Where does your capital stack up against other investors in the deal?
  - ○ Will you lead, co-lead, or take no lead?
- Follow-ons/reserves — Will you make investments at a later stage, in a company you have previously invested in?
  - ○ Is there a minimum traction or growth metric the investment must attain for you to follow-on?
  - ○ Is there a maximum valuation cap at which you cannot follow-on due to the investment price being too high?
  - ○ How much capital will you allocate for follow-on reserves?
    - ▪ Follow-on reserves can range from 0% to 70% of the fund for follow-ons when your investment moves to its next fundraising round (depending upon the strategy of the fund), so there is a wide band of options
    - ▪ The amount of reserves that you hold is dependent upon the size of your fund, the stage of the intended investment, the target number of investments in your portfolio, and your return model

- Pro rata/Co-investment policy — Will you have pro rata rights, which are the right, but not the obligation, to invest in those future funding rounds? Will you upsize your investment in future funding rounds?
  - Will you include a pro rata right of first refusal in your investment term sheets, which outline the conditions under which an investment will be made?
  - Have you considered additional capital sources for pro rata investing partners?

Step #12

Goal: Establish Portfolio Management Guidelines

- Portfolio maintenance and management — How often will you review your portfolio?
  - Monthly
  - Weekly
  - Other
- Portfolio performance — What are your portfolio performance goals? How often will you track?
  - Select a type of metric, such as Return on Investment (ROI), Internal Rate of Return (IRR), Multiple on Invested Capital (MOIC), Distributions to Paid-in Capital (DPI), Residual Value to Paid-in Capital (RVPI), and/or Total Value to Paid-in Capital (TVPI)
- Choose a frequency of reporting; quarterly and annually are typical

Step #13

Goal: Define External Service Providers

- Hire a fund formation lawyer. It is important to note that, in addition to fund formation, fund managers typically use separate law firms for investment term sheets, contracts, employment matters, and more. This could be for cost-saving measures or for delegating expertise.
- Hire auditors/accountants
- Hire other key service providers such as fund administrators, banking providers

Step #14

Goal: Seek Soft Commitments

- Speak with potential investors to garner interest and establish soft commitment traction ahead of your full fundraise

Step #15

Goal: Set Fundraising Parameters

- Set clear timelines for fundraising:
  - On average, the time it takes to raise a fund is 12 to 18 months[8]
- Identify the number of closings, one or multiple, and subsequent closing amounts
- Identify the number of investors

> **Step #16**
>
> **Goal: Create a Pitch Deck**
>
> - Create a pitch deck that highlights your strengths and investment thesis

As a new fund manager, it is critical to configure your fund's basic setup *before* you begin fundraising and investing. Ahead of launching your fund, be sure to clearly define the elements that will determine the DNA of your fund, including your specific investment thesis, philosophy for investing, and expected portfolio composition. Try to understand the terrain of the existing marketplace, such as the available entry points, the competitive landscape, and how existing participants chose to act, so you may use this information as a long-term framework for your fund's structure and operations.

Scan this QR code

or visit

https://www.venturefundblueprint.com/blueprints/fundpreparation

to see the interactive workbook and learn more about
The Venture Fund Blueprint

Appendix

2.1 Fund Preparation Example — Andreessen Horowitz[9]

Review the following example of fund preparation from firms that have walked this path before you. Use the example to help you prepare for your own fund.

Type	Consumer and enterprise technology
Stage	Multi-stage
Fund I Size	$300mm
Fund Model	Target 15 to 20 early-stage deals at $20mm invested/reserved per company Remainder in later-stage investment opportunities and seed investments Number of new investments per year: Target a 2 to 2.5-year primary deployment cycle Average check size: Early-stage venture deals $6 to $10mm initially Later-stage deals $15 to $45mm per deal. Seed investments $50k to $4mm
Investment Thesis	Software is eating the world. We view software as a broad horizontal technology that has impacted and will continue to impact many industry domains. We see our job as being in front of all of the most interesting software-based entrepreneurs and being open-minded enough to determine whether the intersection of software with a specific industry domain creates a ripe venture investment opportunity.
Follow-Ons	Yes

Appendix

2.2 Fund Preparation Example — Precursor Ventures[10]

Review the following example of fund preparation from firms that have walked this path before you. Use the example to help you prepare for your own fund.

Type	Generalist (options are generalist, thematic, thesis-driven, sector-focused)
Stage	Pre-seed, seed
Fund I Size	$15.2mm
Fund Model	Number of portfolio companies: 75 Number of new investments/year: 25 Average check size: $250k Sector: All, minus deep tech
Team	Managing Partner, Senior Associate
Investment Thesis	We invest in people over product at the earliest stage of the entrepreneurial journey.
Follow-Ons	Yes

NOTES

Chapter 3
Fundraising

Chapter 3
Fundraising

Fundraising for the Win

Fundraising may be the hardest part of being a fund manager — it is the act of asking investors for capital, which takes time, energy, and perseverance. The industry average for first-time fund managers to complete, or "close," a fundraise is 12 to 18 months,[11] or perhaps longer if you are switching industries or conducting multiple closings. During a fundraising process, your goal is to convince people to invest in your fund rather than other alternatives, so you must communicate what differentiates your investment thesis from the rest.

In our experience, the key to a successful fundraise is starting the process with abundant preparation, stamina, and patience, while building strong relationships with investors over time. You must stay focused in every fundraising meeting, pitch, and interaction, with the intention of creating momentum. A yes from one investor can be contagious and tends to generate more commitments from other investors. Similarly, having an anchor investor commit early, especially one who will allow you to speak of their fund commitment, can convey strong conviction in you and can help produce positive momentum to propel you toward closing your fund more quickly and hitting your desired target.

Consider how to motivate your investors to close in a timely manner and factor in investor psychology to your fundraising plans. For example, it is far better to state that you are raising a $50 million fund and later increase the size to a $70 million maximum due to overwhelming demand than to state that you are targeting a $70 million fund and fall short at $50 million. The latter can be seen as a negative market signal, indicating a shortfall rather than showcasing the accomplishment of $50 million entrusted to your care.

Whether you are an expert or are fundraising for the first time, give yourself the best chance of lasting through the marathon of fundraising by following an organized process. Fundraising is a delicate balance of pitching your achievements, pitching your future ideas, and pitching yourself.

This chapter outlines key elements of the fundraising process and provides insights and best practices for creating an organized process that is tailored to your fund.

Fundraising Plan for Fund Managers

When you are ready to begin the fundraising process for your fund, following methodical steps can boost your efficiency while streamlining your efforts — saving you time and resources along the way. The following are the suggested steps to use while fundraising; however, the timeline presented is rather ambitious and assumes pre-existing investor relationships, thus, do not be discouraged if the process moves at a slower pace for your fund.

Month 1

Goal: Build a Lead List

- Build a "friendlies" list of people whose insights you value and who would give you direct and insightful feedback on your pitch; this list should not be high-stakes pitches but rather a pitching sandbox to get started, warm up, and work out any rough patches in your story
- Build a long "lead list" of investors from whom you would like to target raising capital
- Build a list of people, known as "gateways," who can introduce you to potential investors — including industry contacts, friends, family, ex-coworkers, bankers, lawyers, corporates, fund managers, advisors, and peers
- Thoroughly search your personal databases, including LinkedIn, contacts, email list, and alumni networks
- Find similarities across investors and then seek more leads with those characteristics, including location and community

Month 1

Goal: Prepare to Fundraise

- Determine who will be your fundraising point person; typically this will be your team's most senior investment professional
- Begin speaking with fund formation lawyers and engage one early in the process

Month 1

Goal: Build a Lead List

- Build a "friendlies" list of people whose insights you value and who would give you direct and insightful feedback on your pitch; this list should not be high-stakes pitches but rather a pitching sandbox to get started, warm up, and work out any rough patches in your story
- Build a long "lead list" of investors from whom you would like to target raising capital
- Build a list of people, known as "gateways," who can introduce you to potential investors — including industry contacts, friends, family, ex-coworkers, bankers, lawyers, corporates, fund managers, advisors, and peers
- Thoroughly search your personal databases, including LinkedIn, contacts, email list, and alumni networks
- Find similarities across investors and then seek more leads with those characteristics, including location and community

Month 1

Goal: Prepare to Fundraise

- Determine who will be your fundraising point person; typically this will be your team's most senior investment professional
- Begin speaking with fund formation lawyers and engage one early in the process

Months 1-3

Goal: Confirm References

- Confirm that your references will be comfortable sharing details about your past investment roles or previous track record when called upon and that they will be available during your fundraising process
- Give your references an outline or an idea of what key points to highlight about you when they speak with your prospective investors

Months 2-3

Goal: Create Fundraising Materials

- Use your investment thesis and story to inform your materials
- Create your pitch deck
- Create an abbreviated teaser deck, which may be three to six slides from your pitch deck
- Prepare additional documents, such as a non-disclosure agreement (NDA), detailed track record, and other data room diligence materials

Months 2-4

Goal: Identify Friendly Leads

- Identify potential investors who have your best interest at heart, want to see you succeed, and can assist you with informal pitch deck feedback to build from
- Determine if any close relationships, or "warm leads," could be potential investors, are connected to potential investors, or both

Months 2-5

Goal: Meet with Friendlies

- Get feedback from friendlies on your proposed pitch deck, investment thesis, and fund model
- Use this opportunity to welcome honest, authentic, and direct feedback, even if difficult or not what you want to hear, as it will make your pitch and your offering stronger and better
- Consider implementing friendly feedback, especially if you hear things repeatedly from more than one source, and continue to update your pitch deck if necessary. Consider your pitch deck a constantly evolving document; however, note that not all outside feedback is obligatory to act upon
- Prepare responses to common questions and tough questions:
  - Why does the world need another fund like yours?
  - How does your fund's model scale?
  - How will your fund survive over the long term?

- ○ What is your personal contribution to the fund?
- ○ What is your track record or alternative display of investment expertise?
- ○ Who are your references?
- Secure soft commitments of capital if possible

Months 2-5
Goal: Add to Your Lead List
- Collect introductions received from friendlies and add those contacts to your lead list

Months 2-5
Goal: Create a Mailing List
- Create a mailing list of contacts who have passed for now but indicated that they may be interested later; continue to send these contacts good news about your fundraise every four to six weeks or as newsworthy events occur. Ensure you are not reaching out excessively for small items so as not to fatigue your communications channel or weaken the relationship

Months 3-6
Goal: Begin Legal Review
- With the guidance of your fund formation lawyer, create a brief "Summary of Principal Terms" document that outlines your fund structure, terms, capital contributions, allocations, distributions, management fee, and carried interest. This can be used later in your conversations with investors

- Work with your legal counsel to create governing docs such as the Limited Partnership Agreement (LPA) and/or private placement memorandum (PPM)
- Be sure to consult your lawyer in order to adhere to state and federal securities law requirements that restrict how and to whom you may offer fund interests
- Communicate with your lawyer the minimum amount needed to raise for a first close, which will be a percentage of the entire fund if you decide to do multiple closings within the same fund

Months 5-7
Goal: Meet with Potential Anchor Investors
- Identify and meet with potential anchor investors
- In general, fund managers will have only one anchor investor but may need to meet with four or five potential anchor investors to secure a commitment

Months 5-8
Goal: Meet with Potential Investors
- Meet with potential investors to continue filling up your round before the closing date
- Consider hosting lunches/dinners/talks/events, virtually and in-person, to soft pitch or secure commitments from potential investors

Months 6-8

Goal: Secure Anchor Investor

- Select and secure your anchor investor
- Confirm your anchor investor's commitment in writing over email
- Communicate the timing of the fund's Limited partnership Agreement (LPA), which will serve as the primary governing document of the fund; for example, the LPA will be sent by your lawyer within 30 to 60 days

Months 6-18

Goal: Secure Other Potential Investors

- Inform other potential investors of your anchor investor's commitment and push for their decisions
- Secure commitments from all other potential investors

Months 6-18

Goal: Create a Communications Strategy

- Follow up with investors regularly to provide updates, for example every two to four weeks
- Send both existing and potential investors any recent good news; best practices suggest that you should manage your correspondence with them as you would manage a "drip campaign," or a campaign where you recurrently send small notes via email to stay in touch and keep the relationships warm

- Send investors any recent press releases created by either you or an external PR/media team, such as existing portfolio company exits, portfolio company success stories, or feature pieces on your fund
- Note that hiring external PR/media is generally considered expensive and often leads to raising awareness about your fund rather than raising money for your fund, so ensure that your budget and expectations are clear

Prior to Closing
Goal: Open Bank Accounts
- Open bank accounts with a banking firm to hold future capital

Prior to Closing
Goal: Engage a Fund Administrator
- Engage your fund administrator if you intend to use one

Month 18
Goal: Conduct Initial Closing of the Fund
- Work with your lawyer to conduct the initial closing and send final legal documents to investors

Months 18-30
Goal: Conduct Additional Closings of the Fund
- If you have not hit your target fundraise amount in your initial closing, work with your lawyer to conduct additional closings

After Final Closing

Goal: Schedule Press

- Schedule press releases timed around the closing
  of your fund

Fundraising Tips

During your fundraising process, keep in mind the following useful tips to give yourself an edge.

Managing Leads[12]
- Ask for introductions and expand your network of relationships long before you offer your fund.
- Build a lead pipeline of 6x to 8x the capital required; for example, if you are raising $50 million, meet with $300 million to $400 million worth of capital.
- Prioritize picking the right partners as investors rather than getting stuck with who is available. You are best served in working with investors who believe in your vision and strategy.
- Remember that your potential investors do not share your timeline or sense of urgency. For example, many institutional investors are fully booked on their annual allocations by the end of the first quarter. Therefore, you should build plenty of time into your process to allow an investor to get to know you, conduct diligence, go to their investment committee, and so on. It cannot be overemphasized that relationships take time.
- Use tools such as LinkedIn, Crunchbase, AngelList, and Twitter to assist in expanding your network relationships.

Collecting Introductions
- Find a path to connect with your leads. Finding a "warm" mutual connection to introduce you is preferable if you can get it. While

there are stories of cold introductions working, you should stack the odds of success in your favor.

- Gather referrals to investors from other successful, trusted fund managers.
- Some fellow fund managers may share leads, if they are not directly competitive. Note that you can revisit the ten or more fund managers with whom you previously spoke to learn about the industry, as now is a good time to go back to those contacts asking for their recommendations, particularly if the fund managers are not operating in a competitive space.
- Once you are introduced to the lead, go for the senior decision-maker, as it is nearly impossible to advance to the senior decision-maker much later. Working with a decision-maker will help reduce back-and-forth and result in a higher probability of investment.
- Keep a detailed list of contacts you have met or spoken with, the date, and the topic for each investor, with detailed notes and any follow-up actions.

Picking the Right Investor(s)

- People like to do business with people they know; build relationships with investors long before you start fundraising; do not let your first meeting be the time you are asking for money.
- Qualify your leads. Ask yourself if the potential investor allocates to your fund's stage, sector, and geographical focus.
- Investigate whether the potential investor has competitive or perceived competitive funds in their portfolio, including other funds of similar size, stage, and investment thesis. Will you be

competing for deals? Do they do competitive investing? Some investors have a thesis in the space, so they concentrate their exposure, and others will not invest if there is any perception of overlap.

- Understand whether the potential investor will "lead" or "follow." For example, will they be an anchor investor, commit early, or only participate once others are in? Anchor investors are often critical to boosting fundraising momentum for a first-time fund.

- Understand the timing of the potential investor and do not let them slow your momentum. Ask yourself whether they will be a better second close candidate or whether they are not really interested at all.

- Do your due diligence on potential investors; this is a two-way relationship, and you must ensure that they are the right part-ner for you.

- Find investors who like you and who have an interest in your type of fund; spend time vetting names; find out what other people are saying about them.

- Look for more than just money in an investor; you are looking for people whom you respect and with whom you can build a relationship.

- Remember you are in the driver's seat, even if it does not always feel like it!

Gaining Momentum in Meetings

- Pack in meetings to build momentum by stacking them closely within the same weeks or months.

- Take as many meetings as you can yourself, as the foundation for a trusted relationship between fund managers and investors is usually set during the fundraising process and initial interactions.
- Although there is a role to be played by placement agents who assist in fundraising on your behalf, they cannot fully convey your fund as well as you can. They usually expect to be compensated based on the percentage of new money raised, so it might make sense to initially meet investors before considering whether to hire a placement agent.
- Evaluate the time you will spend in meetings. Ask yourself if there are too many decision-makers. Are there more than two meetings needed before a yes? Is the investor uncomfortable with a first-time manager?
- Be sure to follow up after every meeting; do not expect the potential investor to do the work for you.

Managing Your Process Efficiently

- After each meeting, reflect on your pitch and presentation to refine your storytelling. While those refinements may not mean that you make significant changes to the actual words in your deck, for the reasons noted previously, they will greatly improve the effectiveness of your presentation.
- Use a self-created database or proprietary customer relationship management (CRM) system to manage your process, such as Affinity, Airtable, Google Sheets, or Pipedrive.
- Determine your first close date versus your last close date timeline ahead of time.

- Be mindful that if you prioritize speed, your total raise amount may decline.
- If applicable, utilize distinct marketing channels to further differentiate yourself, for example, videos and blogs.

Maximizing Your Fundraising Targets
- Set ownership targets, especially if securing an anchor investor.
- Feel comfortable increasing your minimum check size over time.

Public Fundraises
- As a slightly different, less common path to fundraising, some fund managers perform public fundraises if they have a social following to leverage. A public fundraise, such as Regulation CF (Reg CF), is a Securities and Exchange Commission (SEC) rule that allows companies to raise $5 million through crowdfunding over a one-year period.[13]
- It may be challenging to verify each individual's status as a qualified investor, which could have legal ramifications or unwind your entire fundraising round.
- Be mindful of opening your fundraise to individuals you do not know, as it only takes one hostile investor to use up unnecessary time or spread negativity across your entire investor group.

How to Make a Pitch Deck

As a fund manager looking to fundraise, a pitch deck is a necessity. Pitch decks serve as a quick overview of your fund, your strengths, your investment thesis, and your plan for the raise. This allows you to communicate clearly and succinctly with potential investors, while acting as a forcing function to streamline your internal messaging. As Foundry Group Principal Jaclyn Hester put it, "Fundraising is story-telling. Fund managers often struggle with building a compelling narrative that makes limited partners (LPs) want to dig in and learn more. Your job in the first meeting is to get a second meeting."

Your pitch deck should distinctly answer the question "Why does the world need yet another fund?" by addressing your investment thesis, track record, and strategy. You can use your pitch deck to start a conversation with potential investors and pique their interest, which means the pitch deck should not become a dense 40-slide manuscript.

In addition to your pitch deck, you may want to create an abbreviated "teaser deck," containing three to six of the most visual and concise slides from your pitch deck. You can use your teaser deck for select preliminary conversations when a prospect asks you to send your deck. However, it is best to be selective about sending any materials, whether that is your pitch deck or teaser deck, to ensure that recipients are strong potential investors with whom you can build a relationship. Other materials you may wish to have ready, separately, for a pitch could include your references, recent portfolio company news and content, deal flow and pipeline updates, and overall track record.

Here are 13 slides that we recommend including in a pitch deck to best tell your story. Note that the following is a general example for a Fund I:

Who You Are

Slide 1: Fund One-liner. Share a bold statement of what your fund has to offer. This can be an aspiration or a condensed value proposition.

Example:

Why You Are Different

Slide 2: Gap in the Market. State the gap in the market that your fund will address. Mention the special insight you have gained from your experiences, an untapped region, or an opportunity. This gives investors a preview of where you could deliver outsized investment returns.

Example:

THE GAP

We are at the dawn of the Sustainability Era: punctuated by widespread climate distress — which will create the next generation of great companies focused on carbon awareness, water usage, and waste reduction to maintain our planet for future generations.

2

Why You Are Different *(continued)*

Slide 3: Investment Thesis. Reveal how your differentiator gives you a competitive advantage that other funds do not have. This will give investors a better sense of your philosophy for investing and expected portfolio composition.

Investment Thesis Example Template:

> We invest in <u><type of founder or company></u>, by doing <u><your competitive advantage: how you understand, access, own more of them></u>, which results in <u><benefit to performance></u>.

Example:

INVESTMENT THESIS

We support pioneers of this new Sustainability Era, by accessing proprietary scientific research and testing, giving us early insights and outsized long-term

3

Strategy

Slide 4: Fund Overview. A snapshot of the most important details of your fund. Give the investor a glimpse of what to expect in the rest of the pitch deck to grab their attention. Your highlights might include fund size, number of investments, stage, initial check size, industry/sector, location, target company ownership, or number of exits/markups (if any). You will likely repeat this information later in other slides.

Example:

```
┌──────────────────────────────────────────────────────────────┐
│                                                                │
│                        FUND OVERVIEW                           │
│                                                                │
│                                                                │
│     • 24 Investments                                           │
│                                                                │
│     • Initial Check Size = $1M average initial                 │
│       (with expectation of $1-3M overage follow-on)            │
│                                                                │
│     • Sectors = 60% AgTech; 30% Supply Chain; 10% Mobility     │
│                                                                │
│     • Locations = 50% in SF Bay Area; 25% in NYC; 25% Europe   │
│                                                                │
│                                                                │
│                                                              4 │
└──────────────────────────────────────────────────────────────┘
```

Strategy *(continued)*

Slide 5: Deal Sourcing. Where your deal flow will come from now and how you will continue that stream in the future. For example: Do you leverage accelerators? Do you track startups using software? Do you have a venture scout program? Note that many funds receive deal flow from similar, credible channels, such as YC or Techstars, so be sure to set yourself apart.

Example:

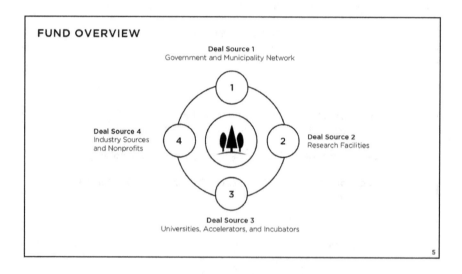

Strategy *(continued)*

Slide 6: Investment Process. Demonstrate how you decide to invest in a company. Condense the explanation of your diligence and selection processes into a few simple steps or a diagram. This shows your investors that you will use a thoughtful approach to select winners.

Example:

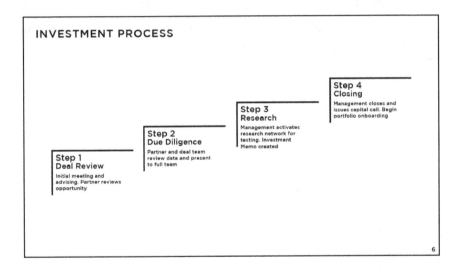

Strategy *(continued)*

Slide 7: Fund Model / Structure. Detail the minimum viable amount of capital needed to achieve your fund's investment thesis. The portfolio model should answer whether you have enough bandwidth to support the strategy and how you scale (if that is a goal of the fund). Portfolio models include such items as the size of your fund, the number of investments you will make, the size of each investment, follow-ons, alternative investments, co-investments, and fees and expenses that will reduce your investable capital. Investors will often ask for your portfolio model to understand how their capital will be managed over the lifetime of the fund.

Example:

FUND MODEL: $3M; 12 INVESTMENTS

Round	# of Investments	Fund Investment	Fund Investment
Seed	24	$1M	40%
Series A (follow on)	16	$1M	27%
Series B (follow on)	10	$2M	33%

TOTAL OWNERSHIP GOAL: ≥5% POST-SERIES A

Proof of Success

Slide 8: Track Record / Performance. Data that shows your past performance. Demonstrate that you have made great investments and/or have returns on prior investments. You should also include your number of years investing, prior experience at a fund, or previous angel deals. For many first-time fund managers, it is likely that angel and private deals, or companies where you coached and advised them, will be most prominent; this works so long as you explicitly state the difference. Make sure that you can document all investments and transactions used in the performance information and discuss with your securities counsel how to conform your presentation to SEC interpretations of what can or must be stated and disclosed in connection with presentations of performance information. Ensure that you have permission to disclose references and your track record. If possible, add a financial returns section that shows your past returns — two of the most common measurements are Internal Rate of Return (IRR) and Multiple on Invested Capital (MOIC).

Proof of Success *(continued)*

Example:

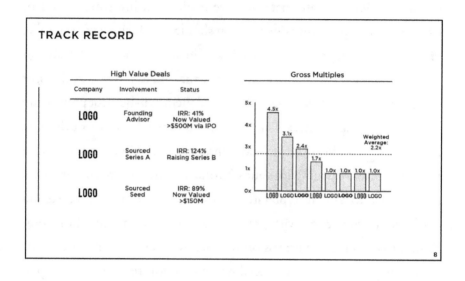

Proof of Success *(continued)*

Slide 9: Case Studies / Portfolio Company List. Display the companies where your interaction delivered positive results. Show their logos along with noteworthy metrics such as their growth in revenue, valuation, or customer engagement. Make sure you can speak to how you added value for the founders and made an impact and where you see the company's revenue and profit potential.

Example:

CASE STUDY

Acme Agriculture – *The leading technology-powered agriculture watering service for farmers*
Gross Multiple: 9.5x // IRR: 41%

- *Pre-Investment:* Conducted 6+ months of diligence as founding advisor, reviewed company's readiness for government financing, used research network to test products
- *Post-Investment:* Introduced company to lead investor for Series B
- *Status:* Company raised a $35M Series A with a significant mark up, leading to attractive $80M Series B and IPO

9

Proof of Success *(continued)*

Slide 10: Team and Accolades. This is proof of both your business acumen and relevant domain expertise for the fund. Include general partners (GPs) and investment partners with logos of their reputable prior positions and education. If you are a first-time fund manager, you may also want to include years of experience in your industry and responsibilities within your fund. Only add advisors if you absolutely need to supplement your GP résumés or create an advisor slide in your appendix.

Example:

TEAM

Greenery Ventures is a team of industry captains across agriculture, government, and tech, coming together to create a full-suite investment

Ayo Neptune
GENERAL PARTNER

• 15-year finance career, entrepreneur, and advisor to 900+ companies
• Former Goldman Sachs, fund manager strategist
• Founder & CEO of Planetary Research Labs
• BA in Economics (Harvard)

LOGO *Logo* LOGO

Mars Hernandez
GENERAL PARTNER

• 10-year academic career in environmental sciences
• Former Venture Partner at Solar Venture Capital
• BA in Biology (Duke)

LOGO *Logo* LOGO

10

Current Landscape

Slide 11: Fee Structure. Inform the investor of their financial obligations to the fund. Although there may be variations across fund managers, most funds generally share a similar structure: the investor typically pays a carry fee to the fund for the general partners — standard carry is 20%; however, some funds take up to 30% based on their specialty and track record — plus a management fee to the management company for providing administrative services to the fund — standard management fees are 2% or 2.5%. Some fund managers also include expected Return on Investment (ROI) for your investor, as they will want to know you can deliver a fund which makes their investment worthwhile. On average, investor expectations for venture capital are a 3x to 5x return, but it should make clear that this is an aspirational goal and is not guaranteed. This slide can also include specifications on minimum investment amounts and timing for your close.

Example:

FEE STRUCTURE

- Fund Size = $75M

- Minimum Investment = $1M

- Management Fee = 2%

- Carry Fee = 20% (of net profits)

- Final Close = June 30, 2021

11

Current Landscape *(continued)*

Slide 12 (optional): Competitors. Compare your fund to two to four competitors in the space. Illustrate this with a table or diagram, and use the same categories previously stated as your differentiating investment thesis, as mentioned in Slide 3.

Example:

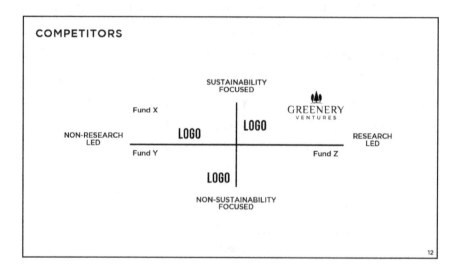

Summary

Slide 13: Contact Info. Include the fastest way to contact you, typically direct email and phone.

Example:

THANK YOU

Contact: Ayo Neptune / General Partner
ayo.neptune@greeneryventures.com

Pitch Deck Appendix. All other more detailed content can be pushed to the appendix. Use appendix slides as visual aids when asked relevant questions by investors, as this helps reinforce your points and demonstrate your preparedness. Common appendix slides include references, sector focus details, investment committee members, press, or extra case studies.

Use your fundraising plan and pitch deck as your roadmap to successful meetings with investors. Be sure to outline who you are, your investment thesis, and the opportunity at hand to get your potential limited partners excited about investing in your fund.

Scan this QR code

or visit

https://www.venturefundblueprint.com/blueprints/fundraising

to see the interactive workbook and learn more about
The Venture Fund Blueprint

Appendix

3.1 Example: Fundraising Advice from Fund Managers —
Hustle Fund[14]

Learn from fund managers like yourself about how they navigated the fund-raising process.

"If you are considering raising a VC fund, I would highly recommend talking with a TON of new fund managers before jumping in to (a) make sure this is what you want to do and (b) get tips and advice. The single biggest tip that I heard over and over from my peers was that they felt that they had spent a lot of time courting large institutional fund investors when they should have spent more time trying to find family offices and individuals and corporates to pitch."

- Elizabeth Yin, Hustle Fund

Appendix

3.2 Example: Fundraising Advice from Fund Managers — Basis Set Ventures[15]

Learn from fund managers like yourself about how they navigated the fundraising process.

"We were laser-focused on finding LPs who aligned with our investment thesis. Our $136mm fund is dedicated to investing in companies that set out to improve work efficiency, including horizontal and vertical full-stack solutions. If an LP needed convincing of our thesis or did not invest in emerging managers, we gracefully moved on."

- Lan Xuezhao, Basis Set Ventures

Appendix

3.3 Example: Fundraising Advice from Fund Managers — Leadout Capital[16]

Learn from fund managers like yourself about how they navigated the fundraising process.

"Demonstrate with unique insights borne of operating or prior investing experience that your investment strategy will change the dynamics and opportunity in the industry and discuss how you will measure those ways. Leveraging one's own experiences in combination with empathy and hard work can help propel growth for each portfolio company. Live your values and your philosophy in your pitch to LPs. For Leadout Capital, humility, resilience, and grit are criteria we believe to be as important in General Partnerships as they are in the founding teams with whom we work."

- Alison Rosenthal, Leadout Capital

Appendix

3.4 Example: Fundraising Advice from Fund Managers — Forerunner Ventures[17]

Learn from fund managers like yourself about how they navigated the fundraising process.

"Think about the most compelling pitch you have heard from a Founder. Why was it compelling: Was their thesis groundbreaking? Did their offering stand apart from the competitive set? Was the team uniquely qualified? Did they have better access to talent, tech, insights? Craft the pitch for your firm and fund with this in mind. What will make your firm stand apart and compelling for Founders to choose to work with you?"

- Kirsten Green, Forerunner Ventures

Appendix

3.5 Exercise: In Diligence Investors Tracker

Use the following to track the investors where you are in diligence with various investors.

Initial Meeting Date									
Fund Name									
Contact									
Location									
Source									
Size of Investment									
1st or 2nd Close									
Next Steps for First Close									
Stage of Diligence									
Next Steps									

Appendix

3.6 Exercise: Confirmed First Close Investors Tracker

Use the following to track the investors confirmed for your first close.

Name	Amount	Entity	Address	Email	Notes	Status

Appendix

3.7 Exercise: New Pipeline Investors Tracker

Use the following to track the investors in your new pipeline.

Status	Fund	Source	Location	Contact	Next Steps	Emails	Notes

Appendix

3.8 Additional Reading

The following can be used as additional reading resources.

- **"Building a Seed Stage Venture Firm," Roger Ehrenberg, IA Ventures**[18]
  - Ehrenberg, R. (2019, February 24). Building a Seed Stage Venture Firm. Retrieved from https://blog.usejournal.com /building-a-seed-stage-venture-firm-c432816ce45e
- **"Tech's Most Unlikely Venture Capitalist," Pejman Nozad, Pear VC**[19]
  - Nozad, P. (2016, February 2). Tech's Most Unlikely Venture Capitalist. Retrieved from https://medium.com /@pejmannozad/tech-s-most-unlikely-venture-capitalist -bb002488f297
- **"How I Raised My $11.5m VC Fund," Elizabeth Yin, Hustle Fund**[20]
  - Yin, E. (2018, December 19). How I Raised My $11.5m VC Fund. Retrieved from https://elizabethyin.com/2018 /12/19/how-i-raised-my-11-5m-vc-fund/
- **"How to Fund a Startup," Paul Graham, Y Combinator**[21]
  - Graham, P. (2005, November). How to Fund a Startup. Retrieved from http://paulgraham.com/startupfunding .html

Appendix

3.8 Additional Reading *(continued)*

- **"What Is a 'Venture Partner' and Why Does It Matter to You?"**
  Fred Wilson[22]
  - Wilson, F. (2010, August 7). What Is a "Venture Partner" and Why Does It Matter to You? Retrieved from https://avc.com/2010/08/what-is-a-venture-partner-and-does-it-matter-to-you/
- **"Some Advice before You Hit the Fund Raising Trail,"**
  Mark Suster[23]
  - Suster, M. (2018, May 6). Some Advice before You Hit the Fund Raising Trail. Retrieved from https://bothsidesof thetable.com/some-advice-before-you-hit-the-fund-raising-trail-73dc646f077e

NOTES

Chapter 4
Limited Partner Program

Chapter 4
Limited Partner Program

Managing Investor Relationships

Your investors, also known as Limited Partners (LPs), will come to expect regular communication from you once they have committed capital to your fund. Given that operating a fund is a ten-year journey, at a minimum, you will partake in a long-term relationship with each investor who believed in you and invested in your fund. An established relationship with investors, or an "LP Program," may include financial reporting, fund updates, engaging an investor committee, managing co-investments and special purpose vehicles (SPVs), or even hosting an LP retreat to create a community amongst your investors.

By keeping the lines of communication open with your investors, your trust and transparency will allow you to enlist their participation in an advisory capacity. Investors can be extremely helpful in facilitating valuable introductions, recruiting, and furthering marketing efforts for your fund.

Developing a Connection

While investors will want to build a relationship with you before committing capital, it is important to remember that the decision is a two-way process, and this is also your chance to determine whether the investor is right for you. Do not take money from just anyone. You will want to perform your own know your client (KYC) diligence process with investors, as they are doing the same with you.

Be sure you know what the overall interaction with your LPs will be. Some red flags to be aware of include investors who are unprofessional, fail to meet capital calls, are difficult to contact, or go back on their commitments.

To conduct your own due diligence on your investors, get in touch with other funds or even startups they have invested in to better understand anything about their behavior that may be an issue. Remember, their behavior as an investor may be different from their behavior as a colleague. Typically, going through warm intros via your existing investors, LinkedIn, Crunchbase, AngelList, and Google searches can highlight any negative reviews or press.

While a supportive investor often attracts more yeses, a problematic investor can cause delays to documentation, unnecessary consumption of resources, or disruptions at your annual meetings — all of which can poison the well with future fundraises.

Communication Principles

Constructive relationships with your investors begin with you setting a standard for the frequency, format, and purpose of your communications with them. As your fund begins to grow, be mindful to continue that substantive, consistent, and transparent communication, which may help maintain trust with investors, even when fund performance is challenged.

Frequency

Your fund's Limited Partnership Agreement (LPA) or other governing documents will typically set forth a minimum communication frequency for financial reporting. Most fund managers should expect to provide financial reporting quarterly, with audited financial reporting provided annually, typically following year-end. However, communication with investors should not be limited to your formal quarterly or annual investor updates alone. Plan your updates in advance and stay consistent, whether you opt for bi-monthly, monthly, or quarterly. As a good litmus test, mirror the frequency with which you would like to hear from your portfolio companies with updates of their progress and performance. Plan your quarterly reporting carefully with your fund administrator and accountants; you may be amazed at how quickly the quarter goes by.

Content

Once you begin to deploy capital, your investors will appreciate receiving information directly from you with highlights on your recent performance and information about the portfolio companies of the fund. Plan to send your investors news related to the fund, publications about the fund's targeted sector, and other related articles as often as relevant to keep your investors involved.

Transparency and Tone

Every communication with your investors is an opportunity to build trust, so use those moments wisely by being honest about your performance — wins and losses alike. Exercise transparency with investors by answering their inbound questions to develop a strong relationship.

Format and Archiving

Investor communications and reporting are commonly sent via email or investor portal, or through a data room. An investor portal or data room can help you control the dissemination of confidential information, archive outdated information, and manage cybersecurity risks. Avoid using platforms that lack clear instructions for access, as you do not want to create a burdensome process for your investors. Be mindful to mark information as confidential if you are sending it via email or providing access to downloadable or printable formats. If you utilize an investor portal or data room, ensure it is password protected so that access is granted only to your investors.

Connectivity to Portfolio Companies

From time to time, your investors may ask to speak to your portfolio companies because of a special interest in a co-investment opportunity, the sector, or general due diligence. Before you commit to making this connection, make sure your portfolio company has the bandwidth and willingness to engage with your investors. Moreover, ensure you are ready to hand over the relationship to the investor permanently, if the investor decides to take over the communication and no longer invest through your fund or SPV. Although this behavior is rare, you must be prepared for the possibility. If you and your portfolio company are amenable to the connection, prepare both your investor and the portfolio company for this type of conversation by setting expectations about availability and confidentiality and by providing each party with relevant information about the other.

Securities Laws

Federal and state securities laws apply to communication with investors. Be particularly careful about future projections or statements of past performance. Be clear about communicating investment risks and do not overstate.

Investor Updates

Sending regular updates to your current investors holds you and your team accountable while allowing for greater transparency. Additionally, committing to regular investor updates pushes you, as a fund manager, to reflect on the decisions you have made, the reasons you made them, their results, and any changes you need to make in the future. The following are topics commonly included in fund updates to current investors.

Summary of Last Period

Provide a summary, a few sentences long, about any significant changes or updates to the portfolio or fund since your last communication.

Portfolio Company Updates

Highlight key metrics of your portfolio companies for current investors, such as portfolio company monthly revenue, annual revenue and new revenue, performance and traction, portfolio company fundraising targets, markups in portfolio company valuation, sales won by portfolio companies, and key hires at portfolio companies. In all cases, be cognizant of the sensitivity of portfolio company information and whether dissemination to your investors would do more harm than good. Remember to consult with legal counsel before including any information about a portfolio company that has filed to go public and is now in a "quiet period" of non-disclosures.

Deal Flow and Pipeline

Describe any updates or changes to your deal flow and pipeline, the number of companies engaged, and companies not selected for investment. This is the stream of companies and potential investments for your fund.

Recent News, Publications, and Hires

Describe any changes to your fund's marketing, public relations, operations, teams, or strategies, including articles written, publications, features, recent news, and hires.

New Investors

Mention any additional closings that have happened since the first closing of your fund to demonstrate continued fundraising progress.

Milestones

Identify milestones of the fund, including milestones that you have reached and those that are pending.

Upcoming Capital Calls

Give your investors a preview of any upcoming capital calls.

Upcoming Events

Provide your upcoming investor schedule, including the next investor meeting or investor retreat. In addition, include portfolio company events that your investors are welcome to attend.

Upcoming Fundraises for New Funds

If you are getting ready to raise your next fund, share this information with your existing investors to gauge interest. By having a preview of your upcoming fundraise, investors can plan their investment allocations in advance. Remember that your existing investors can be your strongest advocates with prospective investors. Be sure to speak with your legal counsel to avoid any regulatory issues that could arise with marketing efforts to non-US investors, especially from the European Union.

Opportunities to Help

Ask for help. If you have established regular communication with your investors ahead of time, you will feel comfortable asking them for assistance. Remember that investors want you to succeed and thus can be instrumental when you are looking for resources around marketing your fund, introductions, and recruiting. Your investors will be more likely to assist if your approach is methodical and patient.

Securities Laws

If your investor communications are distributed to third parties other than current investors and their advisors, then you should avoid disclosing fundraising information about ongoing fundraising efforts to avoid being viewed as engaging in a general solicitation, to maintain your fund's private offering exemption, to avoid being required to register the offering with the Securities and Exchange Commission, and to avoid being required to register the fund under the Investment Company Act.

Investor Annual Meetings

Your legal documents may require you to host an in-person or virtual Investor Annual Meeting with your entire group of investors, plus many investors will expect you to. The purpose of these meetings is typically to share an overview of the fund's performance and future expectations, while also highlighting particular successes and reaffirming your market position. Remember, as with all other communications, it is important to schedule this meeting date well in advance to maximize investor attendance and allow yourself ample time to prepare. Many fund managers will host their annual meetings in April, May, October, or early November, away from holidays and summer vacation, although there is generally no requirement for the specific meeting date. Be sure to check your LPA plus related documents for what cadence of Investor Annual Meeting you have promised or required. The following topics are commonly discussed at the Investor Annual Meeting.

Performance

Sharing performance updates with investors is a positive signal that your intentions and execution are aligned with their investment objectives. The SEC imposes requirements on the format and content of performance reporting. Be sure to work with your legal fund counsel, fund administrator, and financial team on how to present performance information. In general, you can share your performance information in three ways:

- Give a macro overview of your fund's performance compared to its peers,

- Provide a micro analysis of the entire portfolio's performance derived from each portfolio company, which is typically tracked monthly and is most commonly referred to as gross Internal Rate of Return (IRR), and/or
- Present a comparative analysis of your IRR with the portfolio performance goals you set at the start of establishing your fund.

Future Strategy

Earlier, we explained that your "vision" is the desired outcome of the fund, and the "strategy" is the collection of resources used to reach the desired outcome. By the time your first annual meeting comes around, investors will want to know if you are on track with the original strategy you pitched them. Moreover, if there were any slight deviations in your approach due to market conditions or other variables, they will need to know why. Although investors may understand that markets can be variable and volatile, they will generally expect you to stay the course of your strategy so that they can manage their own portfolios accordingly. It is not common for a fund's investment strategy to change, as it is typically set forth in the LPA and agreed upon with the investors. However, it is essential to communicate these adjustments clearly with your investors, who placed their bets on the investment strategy that you set forth and your ability to execute on it. While pivots and changes may occur based on market volatility and technological leaps, your ability to communicate effectively with your investors on these topics will impact your long-term success. You should only consider adding future strategies as a topic of your annual meeting if you have already had extensive discussions with your investors or the Limited Partner Advisory Committee (LPAC) about strategy changes. Nothing, however, should be a "surprise" when communicated to your investors at the annual meeting.

Portfolio Company Case Studies

To make your fund management more tangible to your investors, you may want to have the Founder(s) from a few of your portfolio companies present at the annual meeting. This is your chance as a fund manager to showcase your top performers by allowing portfolio companies' leadership to describe their successes, why they selected your fund to invest, and how you added value. Investors can see the real people running the companies they are investing in by way of your involvement. Many investors will also ask the portfolio companies directly about you as a fund manager, including questions about how frequently you interact, your availability to the company, and your involvement with the company's management team. If you are doing great work with a company, you will want to foster these communication channels.

Financial Reporting

Financial and tax reporting allows investors to track and record critical fiscal information about the fund. The following are examples of the financial and tax reports you should expect to provide.

Quarterly Valuations and Financials

Your investors will expect quarterly financial reporting, including portfolio valuations. Quarterly reports should be sent to investors by you or your fund administrator. In some cases, your quarterly reports may need to be delivered directly by a fund administrator or similar accountant. Consult with your legal counsel to determine whether this is the case.

Annual Valuations and Financials

Your investors will expect annual audited financial statements, including portfolio valuations and, occasionally, a summary of the fund's portfolio holdings. Your annual reports, like your quarterly reports, should be sent to investors by you, your fund administrator, or a similar accountant. Consult with your legal counsel to determine which case applies to you.

Annual K-1s

The Schedule K-1 (K-1) is an Internal Revenue Service tax form that you are generally obligated to issue to each investor of your fund annually. The K-1 is issued by the fund partnership to each of its investor limited partners. The purpose of the K-1 is to report each investor's portion of the fund's earnings, losses, deductions, and credits.[24] You will need to work with your fund administrator to produce the K-1s in a timely manner and ahead of your investors' own tax filing deadlines. It is critical to communicate your expected timing and whether investors should expect to apply for extensions, and note that investors may ask to be provided with estimated numbers in advance of April 15th if your K-1s are going to be late. Consult with your tax adviser to determine your specific needs.

The importance of developing and maintaining a relationship with your investors extends beyond the completion of fundraising. When starting a fund, raising capital may seem like the end goal, but selecting the right investors and updating them appropriately is just the first step toward a truly successful LP Program. The goal of a promising LP Program is to build a durable, lasting, productive relationship over many funds rather than a single transactional investment. Expect to communicate regularly with your investors about top priorities, upcoming initiatives, and future planning to help realize the investment thesis you originally promised your investors.

Scan this QR code

or visit

https://www.venturefundblueprint.com/blueprints/limitedpartners

to see the interactive workbook and learn more about
The Venture Fund Blueprint

Appendix

4.1 Example: Investor Annual Meeting Agenda Long Form

The following is an example of an investor annual meeting in long form.

- Fund Snapshot
  - Capital Invested
  - Current Performance
  - Portfolio Growth
  - Developments
  - Capital Called, Average Investment Costs, Number of Investments
  - Performance of Multiple on Invested Capital (MOIC), Internal Rate of Return (IRR), Distributions to Paid-in Capital (DPI), and/or Total Value to Paid-in Capital (TVPI)
- Deal Flow Strategy Review
  - Formula for Success
  - Investment Themes and Trends
- Portfolio Company Highlights (Deal by Deal)
  - Company one-liner
  - Metrics: Net Asset Value (NAV), Cost, Ownership, Co-investors
  - Latest Achievements
  - Current Product and Customers
- Portfolio Trajectory
- Fund News and Publications

Appendix

4.2 Example: Investor Annual Meeting Agenda Short Form

The following is an example of an investor annual meeting in short form.

- Fund Introduction
    - Investment Thesis, Strategy, Strengths, and Differentiators
    - Latest Firm Updates
- Developments
    - Current Market
    - Firm's Status in the Industry
    - Fund Projections
- Portfolio Company Presentations
    - Overview of Current Portfolio Deals
    - Key Metrics and Highlights
    - Portfolio Trajectory
- Latest Firm Updates
    - Current Fund Performance
    - Upcoming Fundraise

Appendix

4.3 Exercise: Investor Communications Pro Tips Checklist

While you communicate with your investors, keep in mind the following useful tips to give yourself an edge.

- ✓ Play the long game with investors. Establish a strong, communicative relationship first.
- ✓ Do not take money from just anyone. Ensure that the investor's professionalism and background align with your fund.
- ✓ Remember your early supporters and take extra time to keep them engaged.
- ✓ Deliver timely and relevant communication to investors.
- ✓ Establish a regular cadence and frequency for investor communications. Be consistent.
- ✓ Be deliberate in your communications with investors and ensure they have substance, a clear format, succinct length, valuable content, and the appropriate transparency.
- ✓ Have additional information available for investors, including a portfolio companies list, portfolio companies case studies, and personal references.

Appendix

4.4   Example: Fund One-Pager for Investors[25]

The following is an example of a one-pager to describe your fund to investors.

Explore All Ventures
> Early-Stage Venture Capital
> Fund Size: $150mm (Anchor $30mm)
> Target First Close: Q3 2022

Adventurous Team
Explore All Ventures was launched by Sasha Felina, Jane Dough, and John Smith to invest in early-stage, US-based private companies. The Fund is seeking $150mm of capital commitments. Explore All's anchor investor, a large US-based endowment, has made a commitment of $30mm (max 20% of the Fund). Several additional former Explore All investors are also participating.

Proven Strategy
The Investment Managers have worked together for 10+ years at Artic firm where they developed and executed an effective, repeatable, early-stage venture strategy with proven returns. At Explore All, they will continue this successful approach, including:
- Deal flow through industry relationships
- Active lead investor with Board seat
- Sector focus: B2B, eCommerce, Travel, and Hospitality
- Portfolio companies with $1mm+ of recurring revenue
- $1-5mm investment per company and meaningful LP co-investments expected
- Recurring revenue business models

Fund Name	Date	TVPI	DPI	IRR	MOIC
Explorer All I	2017	2.8x	3.0x	56.2%	2.1

Appendix

4.4 Example: Fund One-Pager for Investors *(continued)*

First Class Explore All Investments
\<logo\>   \<logo\>   \<logo\>   \<logo\>   \<logo\>

Extraordinary Performance
The Fund has a DPI of 3.0. Seven companies are positioned to generate attractive returns with five companies on track for an acquisition. The Investment Managers believe that the success of these investments will result in the strongest performing fund in Artic's 10-year history, and the approach serves as the foundational blueprint for Explorer All I.

Explore All Gain
Within this established and proven strategy, the Investment Managers have integrated several highly accomplished, previously venture-backed CEOs into their team and across the entire investment process. These CEO Partners are deeply networked sector experts and universally respected operators. The three CEO Partners have created outstanding returns for some of the best early-stage VC firms. The CEO Partners help refine Explore All's target list of the most compelling target companies, provide advantanged access across to these companies throughout their networks and former investors, create dominant positioning to win the most competitive financings, and deliver maximum portfolio impact as Board members. Together, the combination of a veteran investment team and proven CEO Partners positions Explore All as the preferred, most valuable, early-stage investment partner.

Investors Co-Investments
The Investment Managers have established a track record of providing access to highly-compelling Investor direct co-investment opportunities. These investments are offered with no additional fee or carry.

Explore All Ventures
123 Rainbow Drive, Palo Alto, CA 94301
info@exploreall.vc

Appendix

4.5 Exercise: Fund One-Pager for Investors

Use the following template to create a one-pager that will describe your fund to investors.

<Fund Name/Logo>
- <Stage focus: PE or VC, e.g., Early-Stage VC>
- <Fund size: size, anchor, e.g., $100mm Fund, $20mm Anchor>
- <Target first close: quarter, year, e.g., Q2, 2023>

<Team>
<Who you are, where the fund originated, how long you have worked together, where you are investing, how much you are raising, how much has been committed, key investors and advisors>

<Strategy>
<Problem, market opportunity, business model, deal source, geographic focus, sector, average investment per company>

<Track Record>
<Number of funds to date and (expected) metrics>

Fund Name	Date	TVPI	DPI	IRR	MOIC	Gross Returns

<Performance>
<Number of investments and exits to date, number of deals in the pipeline, key partnerships feeding pipeline>

<Investment Highlights>

<Logos of standout investments from track record>

<Value Add>

<Comparative Advantage>

<Name> | <Address> | <Email>

Appendix

4.6 Example: Fund Quarterly Report Outline

The following is an example outline of a fund quarterly report.

Fund Metrics
Graphs and tables

Fund Summary
Date of inception
Total fund size
Total called $
Total called %
Number of investments

Fund Performance
Net IRR
Total value to return #x
Distribution return %
Realized proceeds recycled

Portfolio Summary
Number of investments
Median initial pre-money valuation (full deals)
Median initial investment (full deals)
Median initial ownership (full deals)
Realized gain

Appendix

4.6 Example: Fund Quarterly Report Outline *(continued)*

Unrealized gain

Total value

Dollars invested since inception

Dollars reserved for follow-on financing

Total dollars invested and reserved

Pie charts or graphs on sector and stage

Appendix

4.7 Exercise: Fund Quarterly Report

Use the following exercise to create your own fund quarterly report.

<Your Fund Logo>

<Date>

Dear Limited Partners,

We are pleased to present the <quarter #> quarter <year> report for <your fund name>.

<Your fund name> Update

<Insert overall fund commentary>

<If relevant, include short recap of LP events in past quarter and mention of upcoming events and opportunities to interact, e.g., annual meeting, Founder networking event, thought leadership dinner>

Appendix

4.7 Exercise: Fund Quarterly Report *(continued)*

Portfolio News

<Insert any portfolio company news here; usually one paragraph each with 2-3 sentences & relevant links>

Investment Activity

<Include 1-2 paragraphs on each investment with logo header, summary of what the deal is, who the founders are, what you invested when, what round, overall raise, percentage owned, etc.>

As of <date>, Fund <#> has called <%> of capital and has approximately <$> investments held at an unrealized value of <$>.

Operational Progress

<Section One: Fundraising and fund operational progress>

<This is a great place to say "Good news! We have reached our fund target of <$> raised and will be closing an additional <$> in quarter <quarter #> for a total fund size of <$>. We have a good pipeline for the final close and would love any potential LP introductions from our trusted investors and advisors.">

Appendix

4.7 Exercise: Fund Quarterly Report *(continued)*

<Section Two: Overall operational progress for the portfolio companies>

<Report portfolio revenues, headcount, sales traction, growth, accomplishments not reflected in portfolio company news>

Thank you for your involvement and for taking the time to review our progress. Please let us know if you have any questions or require additional information. We would love to hear from you!

Best regards,

<Signatures>

<Your GP name(s)>

Appendix

4.8   Exercise: Investor Update Letter

Use the following template to create your own investor update.

<Salutations>,

<Fund name> has been <status (adjective)> this <period>, as we
have been working on <changes since last investor update>. Our
current strategy focusing on <changes or updates to your deal
flow> has <number of companies touched and passed on>. In
the past <period>, we have <milestones> and will be <upcoming
capital calls and events>. <Fund name> will also be fundraising
for our <next fund name/#> with the goal of <completing/iden-
tifying first goal> by <period> in order to close <fund size> by
<period>. We have begun <communicate specific fundraising
preparation, outreach completed and pending> and are looking
for <opportunities for investors to help>.

Appendix

4.9 Exercise: Investor Update Letter with Highlights

Use the following template to create your own investor update.

<Salutations>,

<Fund name> and our portfolio companies had a great <period>.
We have <portfolio highlights: # new investments, follow-on
rounds, exits>. Also <fund name> recently <hosted/partici-
pated/featured> in <event/article/offering>, which provided
<objective/benefit to fund/portfolio>.

Fund <#/Name> Portfolio Updates

<Name of portfolio company> is a <company one-liner>, which
has <portfolio company KPIs, i.e., revenue, balance, burn rate,
product updates>.

<Repeat fund portfolio updates with all portfolio companies.>

<Name of portfolio company> is a <company one-liner>, which
has <portfolio company KPIs, i.e., revenue, balance, burn rate,
product updates>.

Appendix

4.9 Exercise: Investor Update Letter with Highlights *(continued)*

Since <period>, the team has <employee update/acquired> and is looking to hire a <position> to join the company with <expertise>. <Name of portfolio company> has also <key achievements>.

Appendix

4.10 Example: Data Room List

The following is an example of the components you may wish to include or be asked to include in your data room.

Detail:

- Disclaimer
- Primary contact information
- Investor presentation
- Private offering memorandum
- Market size analysis
- "Unicorn" exit analysis
- Highlighted companies from Fund I, angel portfolio, parallel portfolio, previous firm investments personally attributed, etc.
- Fund returns model
- General Partner reference list
- Network venture capital contacts list
- Quarterly report from most recent quarter(s)
- Due diligence spreadsheet
- IRR calculations
- Track record in form and with comparative indices and disclaimers required by SEC
- Performance disclosure
- List of employees
- Résumés

Appendix

4.10 Example: Data Room List *(continued)*

- Investment committee process
- Valuation policy
- Sample investment memos, which includes three to five examples from actual portfolio companies
- Organizational structure
- Anti–Money Laundering (AML) policy
- Trading policy
- Business continuity and disaster recovery plan
- Information security policy
- Payments to public officials policy
- Summary of principal terms
- LPAs, including all funds, side funds, partnerships, special purpose vehicles (SPVs), etc.
- Subscription agreements, including all funds, side funds, partnerships, SPVs, etc.
- Certificates of limited partnership, including all funds, side funds, partnerships, SPVs, etc.
- Certificate of formation for the General Partner
- Certificate of formation for the Adviser
- Regulatory filings and regulatory correspondence
- List of registrations, licenses, state and SEC filings, if applicable, of fund and management company
- Current copy of Form ADV, if applicable

Appendix

4.10 Example: Data Room List *(continued)*

- Information on federal and state Investment Advisers Act registrations or exemptions
- Exempt reporting adviser filings, if applicable
- Information on 1940 Act exemption relied upon by fund
- Current "as filed" copy of Form D
- Financial statements of management company
- Financial statements of fund(s) if it has been in operation for six or more months, plus audited financial statements if it has been in operation for a full annual report cycle
- Statement on Standards for Attestation Engagements No. 18. (SSAE 18) and System and Organization Controls 1 (SOC 1) audit reports on internal control environment, if available
- Privacy policy
- Bank Secrecy Act (BSA), Anti–Money Laundering (AML), Know Your Client (KYC) screening process information on portfolio deals and investors
- List of pending or threatened litigation or arbitration, if relevant

NOTES

Chapter 5
Portfolio Management

Chapter 5
Portfolio Management

Providing Value beyond Capital

As a new fund manager, you must take on important responsibilities, which include cultivating your portfolio. Too often, fund managers only focus on new deals as "the shiny new penny" or on investors as capital is running low. However, neglecting the seeds you have already planted — your current investments — is one of the largest errors fund managers frequently make.

Your job as a fund manager spans across three main tasks: (1) Investor Relations, (2) Deal Sourcing, and (3) Portfolio Management. In this chapter we will focus on the concepts that make up Portfolio Management. Once you have found the top deals for your portfolio, it is your job to manage these investments and to facilitate each portfolio company's growth. As a fund manager, you are tasked with supporting the Founders in building a company that will flourish and produce returns for your investors — these duties are collectively called "Portfolio Management." Many fund managers overlook Portfolio Management and miss the mark due to neglect, excessive interference, or passing unhelpful judgment. Instead, you want to position yourself as being in service to the Founders you have decided to support. Think of Portfolio Management as the ongoing relationship you build, maintain, and nurture with the Founders and teams of each portfolio company you choose to invest in.

The role of managing a fund has evolved in recent years beyond simply making investments to generate returns and profits. As capital has become more plentiful and more readily available, fund managers have realized that they also need to differentiate themselves to portfolio companies. The rise of the early-stage Emerging Manager Venture Capital (EMVC) and Micro Venture Capital (MicroVC)[26] funds, along with this more abundant capital, has led to the development of value-add platforms. With value-add platforms, funds are not only vying for the best deals based on terms and capital, but they are also competing based on the kind of support they can offer the Founders in addition to capital.[27] Regardless of your fund's assets under management or your experience, you will be tasked with engaging portfolio companies that are extremely early in their tenure and need support from you, as their investment partner.

Cultivate Existing Investments[28]

Part of your job as a fund manager is to provide a layer of tools and resources that allow your portfolio companies to hone their skills and resolve their needs — both expressed and unexpressed. The following outlines some of the ways you can be of service to your portfolio companies.

Provide Resources and Communication

Through your support, coaching, and assistance, you can cultivate valuable relationships with your portfolio companies that improve their performance and, ultimately, the performance of your fund. It is important to create your own standards for corresponding with Founders and assisting them across technical, operational, and financial matters. One way to achieve connectivity is by setting a standard cadence of communication and delivering resources to your portfolio companies, such as a set of packaged perks, referrals to vendors, educational content, and other offerings that add value to each investment. Here are some areas of portfolio cultivation to focus on:

- *Cadence of Communication* — How often will you reach out to the Founders? Will you text, call, or email them?
- *Office Hours* — Will you host open or recurring office hours for your portfolio companies?
- *Coaching* — Will you establish a standard method to teach your portfolio companies how to set goals, fundraise, and recruit?
- *Resources* — Will you host a blog, website, or research database that includes best practices for Founders? Will you have internal guidebooks or frameworks for them? Will you offer them an

expert service provider database? Will you offer or have referrals for Founder executive coaching, mental health, or wellness? Can you provide access or recommendations to ad hoc services? This might include "Design as a service" for product design, "Culture as a service" for team lifestyle, or "Hiring as a service" for people management.

Assist with Future Fundraises

As a fund manager, you can offer future fundraising support to your portfolio companies in many ways. The help you provide can fuel the company's growth and help it stay on course with the intended strategy. This is a significant portion of the assistance you can provide to portfolio companies, and they will often look to your leadership to step in with value here. When your portfolio companies are looking to raise additional capital, you can assist with introductions to peers or later-stage funds who may be interested in the company's next round or sector. Be sure to build these relationships over time and well in advance of when you might need them as part of your fund's strategy. You can also be useful by offering a positive reference to other funds on behalf of your portfolio companies.

Once you have connected the company's Founder with the right partners for future fundraising, you can contribute further value by acting as a sounding board, helping with pitch practice, conducting pitch deck reviews, providing insights on milestones investors seek, making designer referrals, and sharing limited partner databases of investor prospects. Encourage Founders to build relationships with investors early, ideally six months or more in advance of the fundraising round. If you find that your portfolio companies are better suited to raise capital through alternative measures, such as venture debt, you can help them assess the appropriate paths and develop your own relationships to facilitate introductions to those alternative sources.

Additionally, there may be times when your value to a Founder during fundraising is emotional support around tough processes, and you can be most helpful as a strong motivator or source of encouragement. Many points in the Founder journey are lonely, difficult, and emotional, and a Founder would ideally benefit from a strong advocate, supporter, motivator, and trusted confidant in their investing partner.

Help to Find and Hire Portfolio Company Recruits

Recruiting and hiring the best talent to a portfolio company is critical to its success. Finding the right people can take months, and each company will look to accelerate hiring once it begins to scale or has achieved its next round of funding. In order to start with the highest number of qualified candidates, you can be helpful to your portfolio companies in sourcing their talent pool by doing the following:

Make Introductions to Candidates

Help your portfolio companies by sourcing candidates through the strongest channels, which may include your former colleagues, friends, or previous employees. If possible, consider offering a candidate database to portfolio companies.

Help to Hire Talent

Advise your portfolio companies to create standardized hiring processes that can help ensure consistency and speed of recruitment, while simultaneously being thorough and helping to secure the top candidates. This may include describing the company culture, discussing the typical compensation packages, and teaching them how to negotiate with prospective recruits.

Collaborate with Talent Agencies

You may also be of assistance to your portfolio companies by assisting their internal talent management or reviewing job postings on such platforms as AngelList, GoingVC, and LinkedIn. Alternatively, you may wish to work with talent partners such as Guild Talent, SCGC Search, Riviera Partners, and The Sourcery.

Help to Close Candidates

Aid your portfolio company in converting high-quality candidates into employees by providing references and speaking with candidates about your positive experiences with your portfolio company's team.

Serve on the Board of Directors

Many fund managers seek to obtain a seat on the Board of Directors of their portfolio companies. Getting a seat on the portfolio company Board is often a function of the fund manager's relationship and legal agreement with the portfolio company. Being a member of the Board of Directors can be an important part of your role as a fund manager not only for providing regular oversight for your investments but also in establishing a level of formality around the running and execution of the Founder's business and, more pointedly, your relationship with the portfolio company's CEO. If you do not have an official Board seat due to your business model or other factors, you can still build rapport with the Founder by being a confidant for key issues, assisting with Board meeting preparation, or taking an observer role on the Board.

As a Board member, you will interact with the Founders on a regular basis through recurring calls or meetings to assess their performance, strategize on upcoming business events, and advise the portfolio company through its milestones. You can help push the Founders to have effective Board meetings by asking them to speak about their company's trajectory on a quarterly, annual, and multi-year horizon. This information is also critical in your own evaluation of the portfolio company.

Your responsibilities on the Board of Directors may also include informal ones, such as creating a "two-way street" of dialogue with the portfolio company CEO so you are included in the difficult decisions. Founders are often tasked with making major strategy changes to the business, such as downsizing or hiring. Offer to be your portfolio companies' first phone call to help them weather both positive and negative events. This means you must work on the relationship early and often to build rapport, as becoming a trusted confidant does not happen automatically.

Facilitate Corporate Development

There may come a time when portfolio companies need introductions to strategic partners that can accelerate scalability and growth. Consider the following areas where you can add the most value:

- *Introductions* — Can you offer your portfolio companies introductions to strategic partners, potential customers, future investors, or service providers and vendors that will enable their growth?

- *Value* — Where do you hold the most expertise? How can your industry knowledge play a part in the assistance you offer to the Founder?

- *Fundraising and Exit* — Do you have a background in fundraising? For example, if your portfolio company is looking to sell, do you know or can you get to know all the merger-and-acquisition executives at the big acquirers in its industry?

Portfolio Management Models[29]

As a fund manager, there are many Portfolio Management models you can use throughout the course of performing your responsibilities. Make sure the model you select highlights the areas where you can most effectively assist your portfolio companies, both individually and collectively. There are three venture firms known for launching industry-changing movements in Portfolio Management, and they each have distinct Portfolio Management models: Content & Community, Hub & Spoke, and the Agency Model. Although these funds represent popular approaches, they are not the only ones, and thus you may find other compelling ways to support your own Founders.

Example: Portfolio Management Models

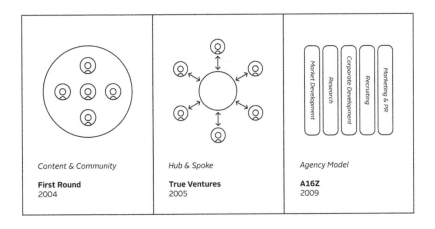

Example: Portfolio Management Model —
Content & Community by First Round Capital[30]

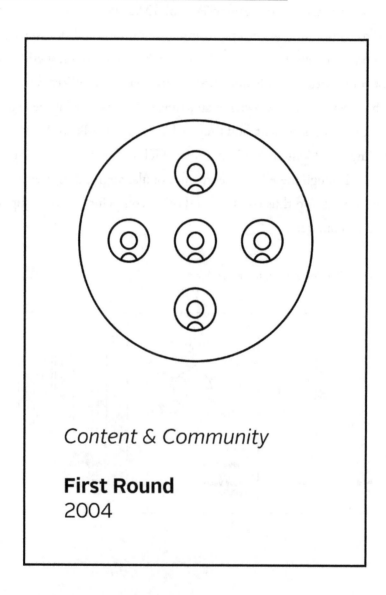

Content & Community

First Round
2004

Background

First Round launched in 2004, offering seed-stage funding to technology companies.[31] They focus on portfolio companies' growth during their first 18 months and believe that venture capital is a product you buy with your equity. Whether it's pre-seed, seed, or Series A, First Round is "building the world's best product for Founders who are just getting started."[32]

Resources & Expertise Required

If your fund decides to use the Content & Community model, focus on your ability to create a community of Founders sizable enough to build a braintrust of information, ideally more than ten companies. You may also need to develop a team of people focused full-time on building products, events, and services that will help connect the portfolio companies with one another — as the greatest outcomes for Founders occur when they form relationships and assist one another.

Products

- First Round Review and Annual Report — Tactical articles featuring advice from the world's best technologists and annual surveys on industry trends for Founders, sourced from hundreds of companies[33]
- Books, Magazines, Research, and Content — Generated research and thought pieces on topics such as sales, PR and marketing, management, people and culture, and product across various industries[34]
- Diversity Initiatives — Published diversity metrics within First Round's extensive content marketing to promote inclusivity[35]

- One-on-Ones — Meetings held monthly where portfolio companies can pitch to corporations, such as Comcast and Unilever
- Venture Concierge — A service to answer Founders' questions, much like a consultant
- Breakfast Crew — A hosted event to establish meaningful connectivity amongst women in tech sales and marketing
- Software Platform — A platform that connects startups across the entire portfolio, with Yelp-like systems for finding recommended service providers, such as accountants, lawyers, and vendors
- Holiday Cards — A holiday tradition to connect its portfolio companies with a video-recorded card[36]

Example: Portfolio Management Model —
Hub & Spoke by True Ventures

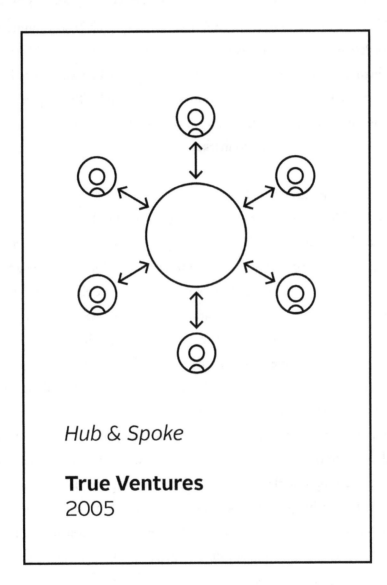

Hub & Spoke

True Ventures
2005

Background

True Ventures (True) launched in 2005 with a focus on giving every portfolio company a direct line to their True Board Member, plus additional guidance from a True Founder Services Partner.[37] The True Founder Services Partner sits with each company upon investment to ask, "What can we do to help you build the best business possible?" while working to foster a culture that "enables open and honest interaction."[38] True aspires to be the first institutional capital in its portfolio companies and is focused on execution along with time to market.

Resources and Expertise Required

With the Hub & Spoke model, you must carefully choose a "Keeper of the Hub" who can establish rapport with the Founders in your portfolio, build trust with each individual, and exercise discretion in all interactions. The success of the Hub & Spoke model stems from the Keeper of the Hub residing on the investment team rather than on a separate operating team removed from the business. This proximity allows the Keeper of the Hub to understand real-time progress and key levers for each portfolio company. You may also want to have special advisors who work directly with portfolio companies on specific issues, such as building enterprise sales teams. You should continually develop innovative ways to solve company problems and dedicate time to sharing best practices with your investments, for example through market research, public speaking, or blogging/writing. Rather than relying on the portfolio company community to lean on each other, as is done in the Content & Community model, the Hub & Spoke model focuses on your fund's interaction with each portfolio company, highlighting the strengths of each Founder and facilitating peer-led knowledge exchanges when additive.

The main goal is to keep "platform" matters, such as operations, connected to "investment" matters, such as Board of Director service. With this holistic approach, support of each portfolio company ideally stays within your fund's investment team so you can remain close to their business, prevent oversights, and have a clear understanding of their unique needs.

Products

- Founder Camp — A gathering of portfolio company Founders for two days of off-the-record conversation to facilitate a peer-led knowledge exchange — a format modeled after Bar Camp and Foo Camp[39]

- True University — A two-day conference on startup-building tactics that brings together Founders and their teams for off-the-record lectures and conversations. The goal is to help teams understand the challenges of launching a company. Most fund managers focus mainly on nurturing Founders, which is a missed opportunity. The University setting is a chance to deepen relationships with the other teammates, develop portfolio company talent, and build your fund's brand with those who may often be future startup Founders themselves[40]

- True Entrepreneur Corp (TEC) — A fellowship bringing college juniors and seniors to San Francisco to work at True portfolio companies and develop their foundational skills. The fellowship setting is a great source of deal flow, talent, and future relationship building[41]

- Resources — A layer of tools, assets, and events around portfolio companies' expressed needs

Example: Portfolio Management Model —
Agency Model by Andreessen Horowitz[42]

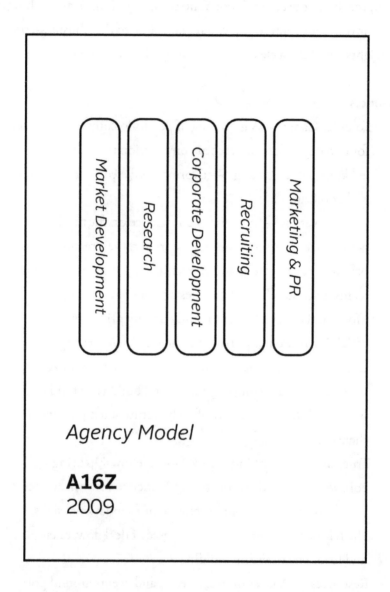

Background

Andreesen Horowitz (a16z) launched in 2009, modeled after a talent agency named Creative Artists Agency that was focused on establishing a roster of high-quality professionals.[43] a16z invests in seed to late-stage technology companies across the consumer, enterprise, bio/healthcare, fintech, and crypto spaces.[44] With over 170 staff members, a16z connects entrepreneurs, investors, executives, engineers, academics, industry experts, and others in the technology ecosystem.[45]

Resources and Expertise Required

The Agency Model may require hefty financial resources to support a large staff to help with all aspects of portfolio company matters. Staff should be able to offer advice on compensation, recruiting, marketing, and more. In the Agency Model, you may also need to build a network of technical talent, executive talent, top media resources, Fortune 500 companies, technology influencers, and key opinion leaders.

Products[46]

- Corporate Development — Advising portfolio companies on financial best practices and connecting companies to broader financial networks at critical inflection points in their life cycles
- Market Development — Connecting portfolio companies with Fortune 500 and Global 2000 companies, government agencies, large private companies, and other technology influencers to accelerate time-to-revenue and create business building opportunities

- Technical and Executive Talent — Building and managing a network of technical and executive talent while making strategic introductions to portfolio companies for key hires
- People Practices — Advising portfolio companies on implementing HR best practices that will aid in the growth and structure of their organizations
- Summit Events — A gathering of executives at large corporations to see a glimpse of the new trends in tech[47]
- Marketing — Advising portfolio companies on marketing and PR strategies by connecting them with agency resources; producing regular activities, including Summit Events, directed at portfolio companies and broader networks
- Executive Briefing Center — Hosting meetings with large corporations, such as Nike and Sprint, where small groups of portfolio companies pitch products and develop business relationships, reaching over 1,200 meetings per year[48]

Portfolio Monitoring

As a refresher, it is important to have a proprietary process for sourcing and monitoring deal flow ahead of being able to conduct Portfolio Management. Deal flow is the stream of companies and potential investments found or offered to your fund.

Establishing Deal Flow: Sourcing and Management

Before building a robust portfolio that will optimize returns for the investors, fund managers are traditionally expected to find compelling investments, research them to ensure they have high growth potential, and scale in line with the fund's investment thesis. Here are some questions to consider when establishing your deal flow:

- Where will your deal flow come from now versus in the future? Will you rely on inbound calls, events, accelerators, or communities?
- Will you incubate ideas and source talent to lead them? Will you operate as an incubator, startup studio, or something else?
- Will you hire a venture partner or venture scout to help source deals?
- Will you establish relationships with key investors who invest at even earlier stages as a source of deal flow to you? Will you work with investors who can co-invest alongside your deals, investors who bring you into their own deals, or investors with later-stage limited partners who may consider investing in the next financing rounds of your deals that are relevant to their theses?
- Will you have a differentiated deal flow channel? Although they are noteworthy sources, note that a large portion of funds receive

similar deal flow from channels such as Y Combinator, Techstars, or schools like Stanford and Ivy League universities. Consider whether those sources are overpopulated.

Expanding Deal Flow: Venture Scouts, Venture Partners, and Entrepreneurs-in-Residence

Another form of optimizing deal flow includes affiliates such as venture scouts, venture partners, or entrepreneurs-in-residence (EIRs) as a way to scale your investment team. Venture scouts typically help bring in promising deals to your fund and have some authority to write checks, although they are generally not considered employees and may have other full-time jobs. Venture partners are not usually full members of your fund's partnership; however, they generally perform deal sourcing, manage investments, and provide Board seat coverage, and they often receive payment through a combination of fund carry, deal-by-deal carry, cash compensation, or subsidies for office space or covering student fees. EIRs may help search for deal flow and are often successful entrepreneurs in between roles looking for a new company to join, incubating a new idea, or getting their feet wet in venture.

Be mindful about deputizing affiliates to use your fund's name and clarify whether your affiliate is exclusive to your fund or not. Be sure to check with your legal counsel and confirm whether you need to inform your Limited Partner Advisory Committee (LPAC) of an affiliate or whether the addition of an affiliate could potentially fall under broker dealer violations.

Make sure you have a customized process in place for deal flow and deal sourcing, as this is crucial ahead of Portfolio Management.

Portfolio Checks and Balances

During the lifetime of your investment in a portfolio company, it is important to establish a process for conducting diligence, governance, and financial monitoring from the time you are introduced through your commitment or capital.

Diligence

Diligence is the evaluation of potential risks and portfolio fit performed by you, as a fund manager. Many fund managers will create a formal method by which prospective companies seamlessly move through their pipeline of due diligence research. Keep in mind that portfolio company diligence can be a significant time commitment, and it will likely be a matter that your limited partners will inquire about in detail. It is also an opportunity for you to create a good experience for the Founders with whom you are interacting; to be transparent, efficient, and respectful of the Founders' time, whether or not you ultimately choose to invest; and to enhance your and your fund's brand by how you interact with would-be investments. Below are points to consider while performing diligence on your portfolio companies. This list is targeted toward the early-stage companies, such as pre-seed and seed, which may vary widely from later-stage companies, such as Series A, Series B, and beyond.

Team
- Is this team the best candidate to address the opportunity? What is this team's unfair competitive advantage? Does this team have deep domain expertise? Has this team put in its 10,000 hours?

- Have you performed a background check and a back-channel reference check on the critical members of the team?
- Does this team have the drive to succeed at all costs? Does this team have stamina, grit, determination, focus, drive, and tenacity?
- If there are multiple people on the founding team, what are their interpersonal dynamics? How well do they work together?
- Does the team take feedback well? Are they the right fit with your fund? Is the team one that your fund wants to work with?

Traction

- Have you reviewed the team's revenue, financials, burn, projections, business plan, growth, customer lists, user numbers, channel partners, business development deals, hiring, marketing plan, and so on?
- Is the product, tech, or service showing momentum?
- Does the traction illustrate a product market fit? Is there market interest for the product, tech, or service? Is there social proof for this opportunity?

Reputation

- Did someone emphatically refer this team to you? Did this person take on reputation risk to recommend them?
- Was this team referred to you by another investing professional? Is that person also investing? Why or why not? Is it out of scope for that investor's focus? For example, a pre-seed deal referred by a late-stage fund where the investment is out of scope is different from an early-stage deal referred by another fund manager that passed because of poor company traction.

Market

- How big is this market opportunity? Is there a clear potential for scale?
- Does the team have a focused, achievable go-to-market strategy?
- What does the competitive landscape look like? Are there other players further along with superior advantages or greater funding?
- What is the exit potential?

Capital

- Do the round size, available ownership, valuation, and terms match your fund's allocation model?
- Is the fundraise amount the correct size for capital required to build and for what the company has achieved thus far?
- What is the intended use of capital? Is it appropriate for the nuances of this business?
- Is there defensible traction, revenue or a clear path to revenue, and a differentiated strategy? Is the business model enduring?
- Is there any innovation in the business model?
- Can you qualify the risks?
- What is the amount of money needed now and over the lifetime of the company?

Product

- Has the team built something immediately usable, known as a "minimum viable product"?
- Has the team spoken to customers, generated feedback, and iterated?
- Is the team using lean methodologies?
- Is the product user-friendly?

- Is the company doing something unique?
- What is the execution time to scale?

Purpose
- Do you want to see this product, tech, or service exist in the world?
- Does this opportunity have a diverse team? Does it have a female and/or a minority protagonist with significant equity stake and decision-making authority?
- What does the future look like with this product, tech, or service in existence?

Governance[49]

Governance refers to a system of checks, balances, and work performed by you through the Board of Directors to ensure each portfolio company is operating in the best interests of the portfolio company's shareholders, including your fund. Your objective, with respect to portfolio company governance, is to uphold the legal, compliance, and regulatory requirements of the portfolio company, which is critical in protecting the interests of the portfolio company's shareholders.

Financial Reporting[50]

The Board of Directors' role is to agree to an annual budget, strategy, and financial reporting with portfolio companies. The Board also periodically, usually quarterly, reviews portfolio company financial progress and makes budgetary adjustments when necessary. The Board of Directors confirms and manages the compensation of key executives, including the CEO. Be sure to understand your portfolio companies' "burn," net monthly cash spend, and "runway," time before money is depleted, so that you may assess their true viability and advise them accordingly.

As a fund manager, ensure that you are providing base-level support to your portfolio companies with the goal of mitigating risks or improving around growth and scale. Consider what unique insight, skills, perspective, or value you and your team have and build that into an offering to assist your portfolio companies as a standard part of your Portfolio Management platform in an effort to establish a lasting brand for your firm.

Scan this QR code

or visit
https://www.venturefundblueprint.com/blueprints
/portfoliomanagement

to see the interactive workbook and learn more about
The Venture Fund Blueprint

Appendix

5.1 Example: Additional Portfolio Management Model — Studio Model by Expa[51]

Learn from fund managers like yourself about how they model their funds.

Background

Expa was founded by Garrett Camp, co-Founder of Uber and Stumble-Upon, to help entrepreneurs create successful startups. Expa cares about the details, from product strategy to system design and user experience (UX).

Resources and Expertise Required

Expa provides companies with expertise, access to a wide-ranging network, and access to capital. Expa is a community of entrepreneurs supporting Founders through expertise, access, and funding.

Products

The Expa partners are operators and builders themselves and can provide Founders with practical advice, helping to craft their brand, prototype, and iterate toward product-market fit. Expa also offers shared office space where entrepreneurs work side-by-side, collaborate, and share knowledge.

Appendix

5.2 Example: Additional Portfolio Management Model — Founder Network Model by Freestyle Capital[52]

Learn from fund managers like yourself about how they model their funds.

Background

Freestyle has been backing market leaders since 2011. Freestyle focuses on early-stage tech companies building soon-to-be massive businesses with something to demo, raising $1.5M to $4mm in their seed round and wanting a $1mm+ investment from Freestyle.

Resources and Expertise Required

The Freestyle team is made up of serially successful Founders now working to help other Founders win. Freestyle provides honest, direct, constructive, and proactive feedback when and how you want it. Freestyle's authentic support means that its team is devoted and dependable even when the going gets tough.

Products

Freestyle has an established network that includes a pool of diverse knowledge and deep wisdom from market-leading Founders and our peers, along with access to best-in-breed resources plus two programs free of charge for portfolio companies to address mental health.

Appendix

5.3 Exercise: Venture Capital Due Diligence — The Scorecard[53]

Use the following outline and fill in sections as you move through portfolio company diligence.

Screen	Metric(s)/Description	Pass/Fail
Fit: Philosophy	\<Overall fit based on fund themes and areas of focus\>	
Fit: Industry/Sector	\<Addressing problem in relevant vertical?\>	
Fit: Stage	\<Company growth aligns with preferred life stage?\>	
Fit: Geography	\<Headquartered or conducting primary business in preferred region(s)?\>	
Fit: Other	\<Additional examples of fit\>	
Quality: Source	\<Cold or warm referral?\>	
Quality: Associates	\<Strength of partnerships, customers, and associates\>	
Market Test	\<Total Addressable Market Size is greater than or equal to requirement\>	

Appendix

5.4 Additional Reading

The following can be used as additional reading resources.

- **"Venture Capital Due Diligence: Financial Valuation,"
  GoingVC Team**[54]
  - Venture Capital due diligence: Financial valuation. RSS.
    (n.d.). Retrieved from https://www.goingvc.com/post
    /venture-capital-due-diligence-financial-valuation
- **"Venture Capital Due Diligence: The Screening Process,"
  GoingVC Team**[55]
  - Austin. (2020, April 16). Venture Capital Due Diligence:
    The Screening Process. Retrieved from https://www.goingvc
    .com/venture-capital-due-diligence-the-screening-process/

NOTES

Chapter 6

Operations

Chapter 6
Operations

Building Your Business Foundation

Operational oversight requires a wide range of skills and involves various responsibilities for a fund manager. You will oversee service provider management, infrastructure, human resources, logistics, technology, and security, at the very least. For many fund managers, it may be more efficient to outsource certain operational tasks to a third party or a service provider than to handle them in-house, especially if your team is small with minimal staff.

Whether you choose to outsource all or part of your operations, you should be prepared to oversee a diverse set of projects to keep your firm running smoothly. Good operations management could make the difference between streamlined capital flows from your investors and to your investments or missed deal opportunities. The overall management of these operational activities may influence investors' perceptions of your competence as a fund manager and impact their future participation.

In this chapter, we will cite several examples to help you dig deeper into the operational tools and service providers that can assist you in developing streamlined processes for your fund. We spoke with over 100 fund managers, had in-depth conversations with a more intimate group, and discovered clear themes shared in this chapter. Note that the vendors, products, and services shared represent only a subset of available options and are based solely on internal fund manager conversations. These lists are intended to be a general framework, not an exhaustive regional catalog, and should not be viewed as endorsements, recommendations, approvals, or rankings. We encourage you to do additional research into each category to find the resources that best fit your specific needs.

Fund Operations

Operations can be broken down into different sub-groups, each addressing a specific aspect of your fund's activities and expenses.

- "Operations Basics" are expenses that come first and are needed to begin your organizational planning
- "Long-Term Operations" are expenses that should be considered after your initial fund formation
- "Growth Operations" are expenses that may arise as your firm expands

Operations Basics

Fund Accounting

Fund Administration

Fund administrators, if you hire them, may help with handling your fund accounting and cash reconciliation. Fund administrators will most often interface with your bank and other service providers or stakeholders while keeping you apprised of your firm's and each fund's current financial state. To start the relationship, your fund administrator will typically lead the financial setup of your fund by liaising with your legal counsel who helped you form your management company and fund entities. The fund administrator begins by reviewing your fund's governing documents to gain a clear understanding of the financial and operational requirements needed to administer your fund.

The fund administrator should ultimately be your trusted partner in managing the critical financial, accounting, and operational functions of your fund. Note that specific functions across different administrators may vary and should be discussed before entering into the partnership. However, as mentioned in the Finance chapter, your financial management duties as a fund manager do not end with hiring a fund administrator. It is your responsibility as a fund manager to oversee and understand your finances.

In some cases, fund managers may work with a full-time, part-time, or outsourced Chief Financial Officer (CFO) who can help to oversee the finances, forecasting, and accounting of your firm or work directly with your fund administrator. Be mindful to pass on tasks or have the correct operational due diligence in place, as you may end up managing finances in static spreadsheets alone, which can be time-consuming and risky.

- Examples for fund administration: Allocations, Carta, Flow, Towne Advisory Services, VMS
- Examples for outsourced CFOs: Greenough Group, Fife Avenue Partners, Towne Advisory Services

Fund Setup

Legal

Your legal counsel will help lead your fund's formation while sharing guidance with you along the way. Your legal team will help balance the competing interests of limited partners, general partner(s), employees, and portfolio companies. As you launch your fund, legal counsel will work with you to design the optimal limited partnership agreement, manage negotiations with prospective limited partners where applicable, and be by your side during the fundraising and closing process. In addition to fund formation, fund managers typically use separate law firms for investment term sheets, contracts, employment matters, and more. This could be for cost-saving measures or for delegating expertise.

- Examples: Acceleron, Cooley, Gunderson Dettmer, Wilson Sonsini Goodrich & Rosati

Banking

A business banking relationship is critical for cash management for your fund. Your bank will hold the cash accounts that are used to facilitate the money movements and banking transactions between your accounts, investors, and portfolio companies. As mentioned in the Fund Administration section of this chapter, if you hire a fund administrator, they may be able to help with these tasks, although they should generally be required to seek your approval first.

- Examples: Brex, Chase, Silicon Valley Bank

Regulatory

As a fund manager, you will be responsible for various regulatory filings related to your fund, such as state and federal registrations, registrations in Delaware, registrations in your home state, filings with the SEC, annual filings, and disclosure documents. You can work with your fund administrator or legal counsel to handle matters such as annual filings, compliance with applicable laws, or filings with the SEC.

- Examples:
  - Escrow agent bank to hold investor contributions prior to closing
  - Custodial bank or broker-dealer to manage fund portfolio assets

Logistics

Office Space

You will need a place to conduct your work as a fund manager, if you are not working remotely. In addition, your office can serve as your hub for meetings, a physical space to conduct business, or a location to host your annual investor meeting. If you do not have an office space lined up early in your process, coworking spaces, temporary workspaces, and at-home offices can serve as alternatives.

Based on your needs as a fund manager, consider exploring the various options, which may include using shared spaces, bunking with a portfolio company, leasing a space big enough to host companies from your portfolio until they are large enough to find office space, or splitting an office with another fund having non-competing interests / deal flow.

- Examples (varies by region):
  - Coworking and shared space: Breather, Canopy, Werqwise
  - Alternative options: Lease space from another non-competitive fund manager, share space with a portfolio company or law firm

Travel

Fund managers may often travel to meet with investors or portfolio companies, if done in person rather than remotely. Transportation related to your firm can become one of your largest early expenses, especially while fundraising, and thus should be taken into consideration as a budgetary expense.

- Examples: Flights, hotels, rideshare services such as Lyft and Uber
- Pro Tip: Consider using airport Global Entry, Clear, or TSA Pre-Check for early access to airports and book your set-up appointment well in advance of your first trip, ideally at least 60 days ahead.

Human Resources

Hiring and Recruiting In-House Support

You may look to make your first hire as your fund begins to grow. First hires are often on the investment side, such as scouts, analysts, associates, or on the operations side, such as an executive assistant or chief of staff. Scouts typically help bring promising deals to your fund and have some authority to write checks. Analysts can take on several support roles, including deal sourcing and due diligence. Associates are typically tasked with sourcing deals, managing deal flow, meeting Founders, and evaluating businesses.

It is critical that you budget appropriately for any additional hire and that your firm has the resources to consistently pay them before bringing them on board. Investors often want to see additional hiring once your fund has begun to scale beyond its vintage year, or the year in which your fund started making investments, assuming your investment thesis permits scaling in this way. As you begin to hire employees, using a job board can help make it simple for candidates to find roles at your firm. Use job boards to help automate and track your hiring process.

- Examples of roles: Scouts, analysts, associates on the investment side; executive assistant, chief of staff on the operations side
- Examples of hiring and recruiting: AngelList, GoingVC, LinkedIn. Alternatively, you may wish to work with talent partners such as Guild Talent, SCGC Search, Riviera Partners, and The Sourcery.

Data Management

Data Room

Data rooms are cloud-based spaces for housing data, generally given to investors who wish to access your fund-related information in one place while they conduct due diligence on you. Fund managers have differing perspectives on whether to disseminate information through a designated data room platform versus a more common file hosting software such as Box, Dropbox, or Google Drive. Data rooms typically include a fund's partnership agreement, deal documents, valuations, and other financial information, such as carry calculations, multiples, Internal Rate of Return (IRR), and net cash flows. If you decide to use a data room, it can also be employed during fundraising to keep additional documents such as a detailed track record or other offering and diligence materials.

- Examples: iDeals, Intralinks, Notion, ShareVault

File Hosting Software

Organizing your fund formation and deal documents will help you to maintain your compliance obligations and to prepare internal and external reporting. Fund managers can use file hosting software to hold key information during the fundraising process for investors along with new documents, such as portfolio company diligence, deal documents, company performance and growth tracking, and executed agreements. Be sure to create a filing system and back-up schedule. For example, sort deals by fund and back up monthly to save time and prevent frantic searches. You may also want to consider privacy laws and other privacy-related obligations when gathering, storing, managing, and using non-public information.

Your legal counsel should be able to help you navigate document retention issues and cybersecurity concerns.

- Examples: Box, Dropbox, Google Drive

Customer Relationship Management (CRM) Software

CRMs are software products that allow fund managers to manage and track relationships with current and prospective investors. Fund managers can use CRMs during fundraising outreach, as they help record each of your interactions through a technology interface. CRMs can be used for not only fundraising relationships, but also for service providers.

- Examples: Affinity, Airtable, Google Sheets, Pipedrive

E-signature Software

E-signature platforms allow you to collect electronic signatures and information, automate data workflows, and have signers use various digital devices in lieu of physical paper. Fund managers may be able to use e-signature platforms for signing portfolio company deal documents and fund-level investor documents. Be sure to check with legal counsel to confirm when e-signatures are permitted.

- Examples: DocuSign, Adobe Sign, OneSpan

Information Security

Fund investor information and portfolio company information are the two most valuable pieces of information in a fund manager's possession. Fund managers should strongly consider information security services to safeguard the sensitive information you have been entrusted with. Information security services typically help protect against the unauthorized use of information, especially electronic data.

- Examples: 1Password, Dashlane, LastPass

Document Sharing

To send, share, and track the opening of documents such as pitch decks or press links, you can typically turn to document sharing systems. Ensure that viewing the information is simple for the recipient by removing unnecessary obstacles such as redundant passwords.

- Examples: DocSend, Slideshare, WeTransfer

Branding

Communications

Communication is the cornerstone of your firm's operations. It is critical for managing investor relations, portfolio investments, and project management with third-party service providers. Communications will take many forms, from emails and video conferencing to in-person meetings. Consider using a cloud-based app when managing your firm's email, cloud storage, and file sharing — this will help you sync the different forms of communication to create cohesion and improve productivity. For periodic or recurring communications, make use of template letters, notices, or responses and be sure to customize the templates as necessary for each recipient.

- Examples: Google Workspace, Microsoft Office 365, Mixmax, Superhuman

Video Conferencing

With a strong shift toward remote work and decentralized teams, video conferencing is a necessity for meeting optionality. Consider having a dedicated video conferencing service for person-to-person videotelephony, teleconferencing, and distance meetings.

- Examples: Signal, WhatsApp, Zoom

Website

A designated website for your firm will often act as your first impression to investors and portfolio companies. Your website should convey your specific brand, instruct your audience on how to reach or follow you, and allow your stakeholders to learn more about your investment thesis and process.

Your firm's website must be well designed, easy to navigate, informative, and current. The content of your website must comply with any internal firm policies you have, such as social media policies. Ensure that you have not included sensitive non-public information, and ensure your website is accurate and up to date by setting reminders to review. You will also want to review the content of your website with your legal counsel.

- Examples: Figma, Squarespace, Wordpress, Webflow

Online Presence

A cohesive online presence helps you communicate information about your firm more clearly to your investors and portfolio companies. There are numerous web-based social and publishing platforms you can use to share general information, your perspectives, or recent articles about your firm. Most publishing or social platforms are free or inexpensive. Make sure that your online presence is consistent with your firm's internal policies. Review substantive content and timing with your legal counsel before making it available publicly so that you do not inadvertently run afoul of marketing limitations, securities laws, or other applicable regulations.

Be sure to register your firm's name and handle with each platform early. Even if you do not plan to use a particular platform, registering early gives you future flexibility and can help keep unrelated third parties from being confused with your brand. Remember that registering your name with a social platform does not secure the name for state law, trademark, or similar purposes. Consult your legal counsel to determine how to fully protect the firm's trademark and other necessary business registrations by region.

- Examples: AngelList, Crunchbase, Facebook, Instagram, LinkedIn, Medium, Twitter

Content

Designer for Materials

An important part of building an identifiable brand for your firm is developing a design aesthetic. Consider using a professional designer to help create your pitch deck, website, logo, media pack, and business cards. Be sure to select a designer who has digital, print, and marketing experience. Always vet your designers by reviewing their past work and, if possible, their references.

- Examples: 99designs, Behance, Dribbble, SketchDeck, Tractor

Copywriter / Ghost Writer

Fund managers may want assistance in developing content for their communications. Freelance writers can be used for marketing or other forms of media outreach that increase your brand awareness and thought leadership. Writers help you create copy for your marketing and communication goals. Remember that marketing materials should not be used to solicit investments from the general public unless you have discussed a general solicitation strategy with your legal counsel. It is important to spend time with your writer upfront to ensure that they fully understand your voice, firm, vision, and strategy.

- Examples: Scripted, Upwork

Long-Term Operations

Technology

Task Management and Collaboration Tools

As your firm begins to grow or hire more employees, you may want to use task management and collaboration tools to manage your personal tasks or the collective tasks of your team. These tools help keep email volume down, while allowing you to export data and documents in order to save the information. Do so regularly if you are processing several tasks on the platform.

- Examples: Asana, Slack, Trello

Cloud Computing Service

If your firm provides database capabilities, for example, a vendor list or a candidate profile list to your portfolio companies, a cloud computing service may be helpful in the setup of your website's infrastructure.

- Examples: Amazon Web Services, Google Cloud Platform, Microsoft Azure

Internet Service Provider

If you have your own office space or work from home, take care to request high-speed internet to provide wireless capabilities. Having abundant bandwidth is critical for fund managers, especially if and when using video conferencing or on remote calls with portfolio companies and investors, particularly when there are multiple parties involved.

- Examples: Google Fiber, Sonic, Xfinity

Phone/Telecom

While a physical or virtual office phone may seem obvious, the choice has implications. Keep in mind that in many states, IRS and securities filings with the SEC will require that a dedicated business phone number be listed. In some cases, the number may be publicly available if it is part of a public filing.

- Examples: Google Voice, Grasshopper, Ooma

Virtual Scheduling

As a fund manager, much of your day will be filled with meetings, telephone calls, and video calls. If you have not yet brought on an operational assistant, a virtual scheduler can be used to set your meetings and manage your time. If you use a virtual scheduler, be mindful of time sensitive meetings where you may need to do the scheduling yourself, and, if you use an automated service, conduct random quality assurance checks to ensure they are using proper professional etiquette when engaging with your contacts.

- Examples: Calendly, Mixmax, Oceans XYZ

Fund Maintenance

Fund Insurance

Business insurance is intended to protect you, your fund, your investors, and your firm from financial loss. It is common for fund managers to carry insurance coverage for general liability insurance, directors and officers insurance, workers' compensation, employee benefits liability, and key man insurance, which covers life insurance for critical individuals on your team. As your firm grows or changes, additional coverage may be necessary. Track your policies, certificates, and renewals through online data rooms, file hosting software, or platforms established with your insurer or broker.

- Examples: Embroker, Newfront, Woodruff Sawyer

Corporate Credit Card

As you launch your fund and expenses begin to arise, consider applying for a corporate credit card. A corporate card can help you and your team manage and track expenses over the long term. Speak with your banking relationship, as they may have beneficial partnerships with credit card companies.

- Examples: American Express, Brex, Ramp

Audit

If your investors require a quarterly or annual audit, you will need a service provider to conduct one for your firm. When choosing an audit firm, be sure to select a team that has experience in your specific industry.

- Examples: BDO Global, The Bonadio Group, Moss Adams, PricewaterhouseCoopers

Supplies, Furniture, Fixtures, and Equipment

You may need to source movable furniture fixtures or other equipment that have no physical permanent connection to your workspace and can be used during ordinary workflow, such as desks, chairs, and printers.

- Examples: Feather Furniture, IKEA, Knoll

Research Analytics

From time to time, you may need an on-demand service for analytical data or research around a particular topic. Research analytics companies can help provide you with meaningful industry information, for example, conducting diligence on company profiles in sectors where you plan to invest.

- Examples: Crunchbase, PitchBook, Preqin, Macrotrends

Growth Operations

Human Resources

Payroll System/Compensation

A payroll system is part of a larger human resource management system, generally used for pay and benefits to centralize and streamline compensation information. Typically, a solo fund manager or two fund managers may not need a payroll system; however, you should consider enlisting one once you add your first employee, as HR matters, such as payroll, benefits, time off, an employee handbook, family leave policies, remote work, annual reviews, and other compensation incentives, will become increasingly complex.

Many fund managers will use an all-in-one system to support overall HR efforts. In addition, you may want to use a third-party service provider to assist with more in-depth HR such as recruitment and onboarding, evaluation and training, compliance policies and procedures, attrition, and turnover. In the case of an employee's departure, your legal counsel can also be helpful with negotiating separation agreements.

- Examples: Gusto, Insperity, TriNet

401(k) Benefits and Health Benefits

Once you begin hiring employees, whether to build out your investment team or your operational team, you will want to consider providing employment benefits that are competitive with other firms in your space. An employer-sponsored 401(k) retirement plan can be offered to eligible employees to make tax-deferred contributions from their salary or wages on a post-tax and/or pre-tax basis. Your firm may also choose to offer matching or non-elective contributions to the plan on behalf of eligible employees or add a profit-sharing feature to the plan. You will also want to consider providing medical, vision, dental, and life insurance for yourself and your employees.

When it comes to insurance, keep yourself and your employees covered for the entirety of the year to avoid unwanted gap fees. Be sure to stay informed through your local governance on which plans are required for your firm size.[56]

- Examples: Gusto, Insperity, TriNet

Branding

Public Relations (PR) and Publications

Public relations (PR) is the practice of managing the spread of information or marketing regarding your firm. Fund managers may use PR specialists when nearing the end or immediately following a fundraising cycle to promote their firm. Before hiring a PR firm or specialist, leverage any journalists or other industry writers in your own network. As a reminder, consult with your legal counsel regarding the limitations of utilizing PR specialists during fundraising.

- Examples: BAM, Bateman, Six Eastern, Onclusive

Security

Home and Office Security Systems

Fund managers can use a home and office security provider for office surveillance, electronic security, fire protection, and other related alarm monitoring services.

- Examples: ADT, Google Nest, Ring, SimpliSafe

Background Checks

Background check providers offer employment screening to ensure the firm has full and accurate information about both portfolio company employees, such as founders, and job candidates.

- Examples: Checkr, GoodHire, Kroll

Scan this QR code

or visit

https://www.venturefundblueprint.com/blueprints/operations

to see the interactive workbook and learn more about
The Venture Fund Blueprint

Appendix

6.1 Exercise: Operations Pro Tips Checklist[57]

While you manage your operations, keep in mind the following useful tips to give yourself an edge.

- ✓ Create a secure document with all essential business identification numbers for quick reference, such as the Employer Identification Number (EIN) and state entity numbers for your various firm entities.
- ✓ Set up regulatory or annual filing reminders — such as home state registration due dates and Delaware due dates — in your calendar to avoid penalties and late payment fees.
- ✓ Adopt an HR policy to establish your culture and share with employees as you begin to grow, such as a dedicated document about your firm's work culture. For an example, see https://jobs.netflix.com/culture.
- ✓ When requesting a capital commitment from investors, establish a capital call schedule that you and/or your administrator can handle operationally. This could be quarterly, one time, or as needed based on what may be outlined in your Limited Partnership Agreement (LPA).
- ✓ You can manage PR yourself, if needed. Before approaching reporters, ensure you have a clear answer for critical questions such as "What are the differentiators for your fund?" "What is your investment thesis?" and "What are your backgrounds, and why are you uniquely positioned to deliver on this strategy?"

The act of fundraising alone may not inspire a reporter to write a piece about you, as there are many competitive firms launching every year, but sometimes an interesting angle can appeal to them. Be sure to target the right reporters. For example, if you invest in consumer technology, pursuing an introduction to a reporter focused on enterprise investing may not be the best fit. A helpful exercise is to find the author of another firm's press coverage that you would like to emulate.

NOTES

Chapter 7
Fund Administration
& Accounting

Chapter 7

Fund Administration
& Accounting

Managing Your Financials

As a fund manager, it is your obligation to maintain appropriate financial controls and to foster fund administration that will accurately, transparently, and effectively communicate with your investors. Financial management is an important part of tracking your investments while understanding the performance and accounting of your fund on a regular basis.

Though financial management is a large undertaking for your fund, there are designated service providers called "fund administrators" who can help you with managing your fund accounting, performance, valuations, reporting, tax services, and portfolio analytics. Fund administrators will also help monitor capital inflows and outflows and determine management company expenses versus fund expenses. When needed, your fund administrator will help you outsource any necessary auditing matters or step in to interact with your fund's bank for business checking accounts, credit cards, and capital call lines of credit. Many fund managers opt to use fund administrators, as they offer opportunities for streamlining fund accounting and back-office processes.

Financial management of your fund does not end with hiring a fund administrator. While it is generally helpful for fund managers to enlist the services of a fund administrator, this does not mean your fund will administer itself. As a fund manager, you must still oversee your fund's financial health. Conversely, fund managers that choose not to use fund administrators are then tasked with managing and reporting their fund's financial position to investors themselves, which, for an emerging manager, can be challenging. In this chapter, we will share some of the key components of fund administration and accounting.

Financial Terms

The following are structures and terms that dictate important calculations for the financial management of your fund.

Management Fees and Carried Interest [58]

Although there can be variations among fund managers, most firms generally share a similar structure. It is standard for your fund to pay an annual "management fee" to the fund's management company, based on a percentage of the capital commitments in the fund. This management fee is used to pay management expenses and salaries. Standard management fees are 2%.

In addition, as a fund manager, you will usually keep a percentage of the fund's profits, known as "carried interest" or "carry." Standard carry fees are 20%, although some firms negotiate greater initial carry on the basis of their specialty and track record that decreases gradually over the life of the fund. Proactively including a standard management fee and carry fee in your Limited Partnership Agreement (LPA), drafted by your legal counsel, can aid in the seamless setup of your fund administration and formation documents, which you can consult your legal counsel about.

Expanded Definitions
Management Fee

This is often a percentage of the limited partner capital commitments, meaning the money you raised, although structures can differ from one firm to the next. This management fee is used to pay management company expenses, such as salaries, rent for office space, and equipment.

Carried Interest

Also called "carry," the carried interest is the percentage of the fund's profits that the general partners get to keep. Your fund must generate enough returns in order to first offset the management fees, other fund expenses, and often limited partner contributions (if outlined in the LPA) before the general partners are entitled to carried interest. The carried interest earned by the general partner of the fund is often shared by the investment professionals who manage and support the fund.

Management Company Expenses versus Fund Expenses

As a fund manager, you must track all costs related to your fund's activities. Such costs are generally divided into two categories: management company expenses and fund expenses.

Management Company Expenses

Management company expenses are used to cover overhead of the management company. For example, employee salaries, benefits, rent, and office supplies are often management company expenses. Management company expenses are costs paid by the management company using management fees and therefore are not paid directly by the fund.

Fund Expenses

Fund expenses are related to the activities of your specific fund and are clearly stated in your governing documents. For example, fund expenses could include legal fees related to the formation of a fund, making and maintaining investments, expenses related to auditing the fund's financials, limited partner meetings for the specific fund, and expenditures for tax reporting. Fund administrator costs are often treated as fund expenses, but this may be a topic of discussion or negotiation with your investors. Fund expenses are costs charged directly to the fund and are passed through as costs to the underlying limited partners.

General Partner Commitment (GP Commit)

It is considered industry standard for general partners to contribute 1% to 2% of the total amount raised as the "GP Commit." Investors want you to show that you have skin in the game by committing some of your own money into the fund you are raising. For example, if you are raising a $50 million fund, the GP Commit expected may be $500,000 (which is 1% of $50 million).

It is common for the GP Commit to be contributed as cash, notes, or some combination thereof. This may already be laid out in your LPA, thus, you should consult your Legal counsel to verify specifics.

Fund Administration[59]

A fund administrator can help perform tasks to track investments and run your fund's accounting. Fund administrators will most often interface with your bank and other service providers or stakeholders, while helping to keep you apprised of your firm's and each fund's current financial state. To start the relationship, your fund administrator will typically lead the financial setup of your fund by liaising with the legal counsel who helped you form the management company and fund entities. The fund administrator begins by reviewing your fund's governing documents to gain a clear understanding of the financial and operational requirements needed to administer your fund.

The fund administrator should ultimately be your partner in managing the critical financial, accounting, and operational functions of your fund. Specific functions across different administrators may vary and should be discussed with an administrative service provider before entering into a partnership. For example, a fund administrator's service offering could differ across financial reporting and accounting, fund operations, investor relations, compliance, capital movements, audit, and so on.

Fund Accounting

Fund administrators, if you hire them, may help with handling your fund accounting and cash reconciliation. This generally includes reconciling your bank transactions and performing a month-end or quarter-end process to verify credit and debit entries. Separately, you may work with your fund administrator to create a process for the best method of bookkeeping, where you, as the fund manager, will pay your own invoice expenses through your business bank account. To track daily expenses, your fund administrator may also suggest that you use expense management tools such as Expensify, Xero, or QuickBooks.

Outsourced CFO Services and External Support

In addition to or in conjunction with your fund administrator, a full-time, part-time, or outsourced Chief Financial Officer (CFO) can help you oversee the finances, forecasting, and accounting of your firm. Fund managers who have the budget may lean on outsourced CFOs in the early years of a firm's growth before bringing the full-time role in-house. Even if you decide to work with an outsourced CFO, it is always important to take the time to personally understand how your fund's economics work and remain constantly informed on your metrics and numbers.

Capital Movements

The following are capital movements that matter for the financial management of your fund.

Inflows and Outflows

You may work with your fund administrator to review and create a process to manage the inflows and outflows of your fund. Understanding your inflows and outflows ledger includes the tracking of debits, credits, and cash transfers. Most notably, the following are common cash movements for your fund, which will be dictated by the terms of your fund's governing documents.

Inflows

- **Capital Calls and Capital Contributions** — The process by which investors contribute capital to the fund

Outflows

- **Expenses** — The process of paying the expenses of the management company or the fund
- **Investments** — The main outflows of cash in your fund will be investments you are making
- **Capital Distributions** — The process of transferring cash or securities gains to the fund's limited partners most often occurs when portfolio companies reach an exit or liquidity event, or when the fund terminates
- **Recycling Capital** — The process of reinvesting realized profits back into portfolio companies

Financial Reports and Statements

As a fund manager, you will need to develop a schedule in accordance with your fund's governing documents to deliver quarterly reports, annual reports, and annual Schedule K-1 tax documents to your investors. Your fund administrator may help you in preparing and drafting these financial correspondences in accordance with generally accepted accounting principles (GAAP). It is important to understand these reports, as you will need to approve them before they are distributed to your investors. Similarly, you should have a clear understanding of when you will issue your capital contribution notices, distribution notices, and general statements. You and your fund administrator should maintain all financial documents as well as other relevant fund information over the life of your fund.

Tax Services

Though tax services vary widely based on the composition of your fund and its investments, you can typically expect tax services to cover the preparation of annual tax returns and Schedule K-1s and/or equivalents, calculation of tax withholdings, and maintenance of tax cost basis. Schedule K-1s report the income, deductions, and credits of your fund, plus how they flow through to your investors. You and your fund administrator may leverage internal or external tax professionals to provide tax support to your fund. The tax support provided by your fund administrator or an outside tax advisor can be beneficial for tax planning, reporting, and compliance.

Budgeting

A business budget can help you estimate your income and expenditures over time. For many fund managers, even if they are experienced professionals in the finance and investing industries, creating a budget may be a new process.

Many new fund managers do not realize the large cost of running a fund, which you can estimate to be approximately 25% of the committed capital over the life of the fund. For example, if you are raising a $15 million fund with a 2% management fee, your management fee over the life of your fund will be $3 million (2% management fee × 10 years = 20%; 20% of $15 million = $3 million). Then your legal, fund administration, audit, and tax easily make up the rest of your costs, from 20% to 25%. Thus, your costs may be closer to $3.75 million over the life of the fund (25% of $15 million = $3.75 million). On average, this is an annual cost of $375,000 to run your fund.

Nonetheless, budgeting is essential in forecasting your financial planning. Building a business budget, especially when launching a new fund, can help you gain clarity about whether you are allocating resources optimally, whether you need to take on additional employees, or whether you need to allocate expenses among multiple generations of fund entities.

Investor Portal

An investor portal is an online solution for you to access and share financial documents with your investors through a secure location for fund administration purposes. Investor portals allow you to have a branded destination plus the capability of managing controls and tracking capital calls from your investors. Portals can be time-saving solutions for your fund, in lieu of spending time sending and responding to emails. Fund administrators may provide portals to your investors, and these can be used to send files safely and quickly. Some investors may prefer this method of information sharing once they are comfortable with signing up for the portal account. Be sure to establish strict security and privacy protocols for this portal and all confidential investor information.

Financial Returns

The following outlines some of the financial returns matters you will need to be aware of for your fund.

Performance

Accurate reporting of the performance of your underlying investments, and therefore your fund, is a critical part of the investment process. You and your fund administrator should track and understand your fund economics, including metrics such as Internal Rate of Return (IRR), Multiple on Invested Capital (MOIC), Return on Investment (ROI), Distributions to Paid-in Capital (DPI), Residual Value to Paid-in Capital (RVPI), and Total Value to Paid-in Capital (TVPI), which all measure performance. In fact, IRR and MOIC are two of the most fundamental measurements for venture investing.

Internal Rate of Return (IRR)

IRR takes time into account to give you an expected annual growth rate.

- For example, and as seen in the equation below, if you invest $1 million and return $5 million in year 5, the IRR is 37.97%. The calculation is $(\$5,000,000/\$1,000,000)^{(1/5\,-\,1)}$.
- However, if you invest that same $1 million and return $5 million in year 10, the IRR is much lower, at 17.46%. The calculation is $(\$5,000,000/\$1,000,000)^{(1/10\,-\,1)}$.

Multiple on Invested Capital (MOIC)

MOIC compares the amount of capital put into the portfolio to the portfolio's current value. For example, if you invest $5 million and the portfolio is now worth $7.5 million, your MOIC is 1.5x.

Total Value to Paid-in Capital (TVPI)

TVPI is the fund's cumulative distributions and value divided by the amount of capital paid in. For example, if you made and distributed $9 million, while initial capital commitments were $3 million, then TVPI is 3x.

Return on Investment (ROI)

ROI is calculated by dividing the profit earned on an investment by the cost of that investment. For example, an investment with a profit of $2 million and a cost of $2 million would have an ROI of 1, or 1x, or 100% when expressed as a percentage.

Distributions to Paid-in Capital (DPI)

DPI represents the amount of capital returned to investors divided by a fund's capital calls at the valuation date. DPI reflects the realized cash returns generated by the fund's investments at the valuation date. For example, if you have returned $24 million of capital and your total fund size is $12 million, with only 25% of capital called to date at $3 million, then your DPI is 8x ($24,000,000/$3,000,000). However, if you had 100% of capital called to date at $12 million, your DPI is 2x ($24,000,000/$12,000,000).

Residual Value to Paid-in Capital (RVPI)

RVPI is a ratio that measures how much unrealized value remains in the investment. For example, a RVPI ratio of 0.60x means that the remaining investments are valued at 60 cents for every dollar contributed.

Your performance numbers can fluctuate on a quarterly basis, as a portfolio company may have a down round, fail, or have a marked-up round. For example, a positive liquidity event or new round with a portfolio company can change your TVPI for a period of time. You might use this information to calculate and provide performance information about the fund to your investors on a quarterly basis.

Valuation

Valuation of each investment will feed into your performance metrics; thus, it is highly important to track valuation changes of your fund's portfolio companies. Be sure to confirm your information rights with your legal counsel and verify the frequency with which your portfolio companies must provide you with their valuations. Information rights are critical with long-standing investments that have raised several rounds since your original funding. The portfolio company may also be providing you with other documentation to update their valuation, including a cap table document that details who has ownership in the company, a post-money valuation that represents the company's estimated worth after investor capital injections, a new shares outstanding summary, their mandated 409A valuation, or any other materials related to a fundraising round or liquidity event closing. A fund administrator may assist you in your valuation process.

SEC Requirements

The Securities and Exchange Commission (SEC) has very particular requirements for the reporting of performance information of private investment funds and investment management firms that apply under SEC anti-fraud rules, even if your management company is exempt from SEC investment adviser registration. Work with your fund administrator to ensure that your performance information in your external reporting is accurate and meets SEC requirements.

Pension funds and other institutional investors often request performance information presented in accordance with Chartered Financial Analyst (CFA) Institute standards. This is sometimes referred to as Global Investment Performance Standards (GIPS) compliant reporting. If you represent that your performance information meets these standards, be certain that it actually does. Compliance with these requirements typically requires use of an external accounting firm or consultant that specializes in this type of performance information. Audit of this information and the process by which it is compiled is normally required to meet the GIPS reporting standards of the CFA Institute. The SEC indicates that misrepresenting performance information as GIPS compliant is a violation of SEC anti-fraud rules.

Banking and Credit Facilities

The following are banking and credit facility matters relating to the financial management of your fund.

Banking

A business banking relationship is critical for cash management for your fund. Your bank will hold the cash accounts that are used to facilitate the money movements and banking transactions between your accounts, investors, and portfolio companies. If you hire a fund administrator, they may be able to help with these tasks, although they will need and should seek your approval before initiating transfers.

With the help of your banker, you will be able to open the bank account(s) needed for your business checking, corporate credit cards, debit cards; plus order physical checks. You may also delegate access to authorized individuals, such as trusted employees or your fund administrator, to manage users and approve payments or to safeguard against fraud. Banks are typically equipped with money-management software, brokerage websites, and mobile banking to make it easier to manage your assets.

Lines of Credit

A line of credit allows you the flexibility to borrow capital from your bank when you need to meet specific working capital requirements. For example, lines of credit can be granted to your fund as a bridge between capital calls, which can help you smooth out capital movements and prevent you from overcalling investors when you are holding multiple fund closings. Generally, line of credit repayment terms are between 90 days and 120 days, plus a total term of 12 months for the line, with the intention to renew annually. The rate for a line of credit is decided by your bank on a case-by-case basis; however, pricing is typically based on prime rates.

As a best practice, be sure you set up your line of credit early, as it may take three weeks or more to open with your bank. Once opened, remember to give at least two weeks' advance notice to your bank before borrowing the capital. Keep in mind that your fund's governing documents, as well as investment adviser regulations, may limit your borrowing capacity, so be sure to work with your fund counsel when structuring borrowings. You may also need to engage a third-party escrow agent bank to hold investor contributions prior to closing and a custodial bank or broker-dealer for fund assets, if applicable.

Special Purpose Vehicles (SPVs) and Other Fund Entities
If your fund has created alternative investment vehicles, such as SPVs, parallel funds, alternative funds, or other unique vehicles, the basic principles of financial management will similarly apply. Many fund managers find the management of SPVs onerous, so be sure to understand the financial processes as they relate to reporting, capital calls, and wire transfers. You will want to enlist your fund administrator and outside counsel to understand the mechanics of your SPVs, just as you would for your fund.

As a fund manager, being well versed in financial management is an indication of your commitment to both returns and compliance for your fund. As each quarter of your fund's life progresses, your performance and reporting will also begin to take shape. Your knowledge around financial management, fund administration, and accounting will help inform your investors.

Scan this QR code

or visit

https://www.venturefundblueprint.com/blueprints/finance

to see the interactive workbook and learn more about
The Venture Fund Blueprint

Appendix

7.1 Example: Fund Structure Drawing[60]

The following is an example drawing of a common fund structure.

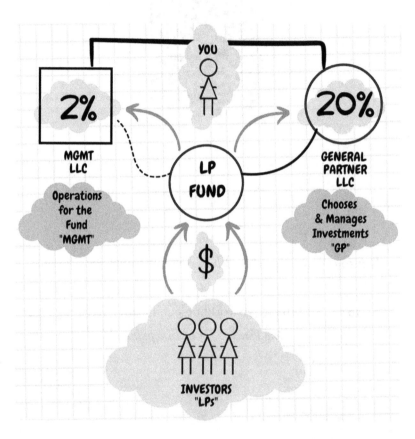

Appendix

7.2 Example: Fund Administrator Services[61]

The following is an example of standard services your fund administrator may provide to you.

Accounting and Reporting:

- Maintain accounting books and records
- Record investment valuations as provided by the fund manager
- Prepare trial balance, general ledger, statement of financial condition, schedule of investments, statement of operations, schedule of realized gain (loss), statement of changes in partners' capital, and partners' capital allocation waterfall on a quarterly basis
- Prepare performance metrics, such as net Internal Rate of Return (IRR) and Total Value to Paid-in-Capital (TVPI)
- Manage payment of fund expenses
- Manage year-end tax process
  - Provide books and records to external tax team
  - Manage relationship with tax team and respond to questions
  - Work with tax team to determine annual tax distributions as provided for in the limited partnership agreement (LPA)
  - Post investor Schedule K-1s to secure limited partner portal as outlined in the LPA
  - Make tax payments as outlined by external tax team
  - Answer questions around domicile of fund structure in partnership with legal counsel

Appendix

7.2 Example: Fund Administrator Services *(continued)*

- Explain matters such as UBTI (Unrelated Business Income Tax), FATCA (Foreign Account Tax Compliance Act), CFIUS (the Committee on Foreign Investment in the United States), KYC (Know Your Customer), and AML (Anti-Money Laundering)
- Manage year-end audit process
  - Provide books, records, and support documentation to external auditors
  - Manage audit relationship and oversee day-to-day process
  - Prepare and review financial statement footnote schedules and language
  - Calculate performance metrics, including net IRR and financial highlights

Investor Relations:

- Maintain investor contact preferences, which can be done within fund administrator's proprietary software or CRM system, for example
- Obtain and store formation documentation, including formation certificates, legal agreements, and individual investor subscription agreements
- Maintain secure limited partner portal, including posting limited partnership agreement (LPA), financial statements, capital call history, capital account history, and tax documents

Appendix

7.2 Example: Fund Administrator Services *(continued)*

- Attend to investor requests, including audit confirmations, data requests, and other accounting or operations questions

Schedule of Services — Fund Entity:

- Manage capital call process
  - Send capital contribution notices
  - Track limited partner payments
  - Send reminder notices
- Manage investment funding process
  - Obtain draft documentation and review for pertinent data points
  - Collect and record underlying portfolio company data
  - Set up investment funding wire for approval by fund manager
  - Obtain executed purchase documentation
- Manage quarterly financial statement process
  - Send quarterly reporting package including letter from general partner if applicable and individual partner capital account statements
- Manage cash distribution process
  - Work with external tax team to understand the implications of realized events, tax distributions, and discretionary distributions
  - Prepare distribution calculation by investor
  - Prepare and send distribution notices to investors

Appendix

7.2 Example: Fund Administrator Services *(continued)*

- ○ Obtain and maintain investor banking information
- ○ Wire cash distributions to investors
- Manage stock distribution process
  - ○ Work with external tax team to understand the implications of realized events and in-kind distributions
  - ○ Prepare distribution calculation by investor
  - ○ Prepare and send distribution notices to investors
  - ○ Obtain and maintain investor brokerage information
  - ○ Work with external brokerage firm to facilitate stock distribution process
- Manage day-to-day banking relationship, including line of credit drawdowns, payments, and compliance certificates if applicable
- Establish connections to experienced vendors, including banking relationships, brokerage relationships, audit and tax relationships, compliance, and insurance providers

Schedule of Services — General Partner Entity:
- Maintain accounting books and records
- Prepare balance sheet, income statement, and detailed general ledger for review
- Manage payment of entity expenses

Appendix

7.2 Example: Fund Administrator Services *(continued)*

- Provide books and records to external tax team to aid in estimated tax payment calculations if needed and to facilitate in annual tax reporting

Schedule of Services — Management Company:
- Maintain accounting books and records
- Prepare balance sheet, income statement, and detailed general ledger for review
- Manage payment of entity expenses
- Facilitate credit card expense reporting process and cash reimbursement process using an expense management system
- Administer employee payroll, input benefits deductions, and expense reimbursements
  - Note: Human resources, compensation, and benefit selection are at the discretion of the fund manager
- Provide books and records to external tax team to aid in estimated tax payment calculations if needed and to facilitate in annual tax reporting
- Prepare annual 1099 filings

Software Platform:
- Portfolio management
- Limited partner management

Appendix

7.2 Example: Fund Administrator Services *(continued)*

- Scenario modeling, including waterfall and next round scenarios
- Responsive software support

Third-Party Provider Communication/Integration:

- Payroll/benefits: Gusto, Expensify, Bill.com, ADP, TriNet, Paychex, Justworks
- General ledger: Xero, QuickBooks
- Audit: KPMG, Ernst & Young, Deloitte, PricewaterhouseCoopers, and regional firms
- Tax: KPMG, Ernst & Young, Deloitte, PricewaterhouseCoopers, and regional firms
- Communication/productivity tools: Asana, Slack

Appendix

7.3 Example: Finance Advice from Fund Managers — 1517 Fund[62]

Learn from fund managers like yourself about finance considerations they found helpful.

"When considering your tax implications as a GP, check with your accountant about the differences between being taxed on an LLC with a K-1 versus being taxed on personal income with a W-2. With the former, be careful of holding unnecessary money in the management account on December 31st, as this may lead to a hefty personal tax liability."

- Michael Gibson and Danielle Strachman, 1517 Fund

Appendix

7.4 Example: Finance Advice from Fund Managers — Forerunner Ventures[63]

Learn from fund managers like yourself about finance considerations they found helpful.

"It will be years before you have real results in the form of investment returns. In the time before then, it is a worthwhile investment to make efforts to build confidence in your discipline and investment process. Use your fundraise as the starting point. Set up a data room, including all the foundations of your own business plan. Document a view of the market and your investment outlook, in particular where you see outsized potential. Offer a team overview and a hiring plan. Identify initial investment and follow-on criteria and note how you plan to support Founders. Share insight into how you plan to access great deal flow. If you have made investments in the past, share your investment memos and diligence materials."

- Kirsten Green, Forerunner Ventures

Appendix

7.5 Example: Cap Table of Unaudited Financials[64]

Use the following as a reference of components you may need for your fund administration and accounting.

First Round of Funding

Pre-Money Valuation	$3,000,000
Amount Raised	$1,000,000
Post-Money Valuation	$4,000,000
% Ownership Being Sold	25%
Initial Outstanding Shares	6,000,000
Post-Investment Shares	8,000,000
Shares Being Sold	2,000,000

	$ Invested	Common Shares	Preferred Shares	Price per Share	% Ownership
Founding Team	N/a	6,000,000	N/a	N/a	75.00%
Investor X	$500,000	N/a	1,000,000	$0.50	12.50%
Investor Y	$300,000	N/a	600,000	$0.50	7.50%
Investor Z	$200,000	N/a	400,000	$0.50	5.00%

Appendix

7.6 Example: Cap Table of Company Valuation[65]

Use the following as a reference of components you may need for your fund administration and accounting.

Company Valuation

	Total Value	Price per Share	# of Shares	% of Total
Series A Pre-Money Valuation	$1,000,000	$5.00	200,000	22.2%
New Equity Raised	$3,500,000	$5.00	700,000	77.8%
Post-Money Valuation	$4,500,000	$5.00	900,000	100.0%

Company Ownership Cap Table

Shareholders	Capital	Common Shares	Preferred Shares	Total Shares	% Ownership
Founders	$0	200,000	-	200,000	22.2%
<Investor>	$100,000		20,000	20,000	2.2%
<Investor>	$250,000		50,000	50,000	5.6%
<Investor>	$100,000		20,000	20,000	2.2%
<Investor>	$1,200,000		240,000	240,000	26.7%
<Investor>	$250,000		50,000	50,000	5.6%
<Investor>	$100,000		20,000	20,000	2.2%
<Investor>	$500,000		100,000	100,000	11.1%
<Investor>	$400,000		80,000	80,000	8.9%
<Investor>	$250,000		50,000	50,000	5.6%
<Investor>	$350,000		70,000	70,000	7.8%
Total	**$3,500,000**	**200,000**	**700,000**	**900,000**	**100.0%**

Appendix

7.7 Example: Cap Table with Existing Debt Notes[66]

Use the following as a reference of components you may need for your fund administration and accounting.

Pre-Series A Cap Table

	Common	% Fully-Diluted Equity (FD)
Founder 1	500,000	50%
Founder 2	500,000	50%
	1,000,000	**100%**

Appendix

7.7 Example: Cap Table with Existing Debt Notes *(continued)*

CONVERTIBLE NOTE (1)

0.703703704

Closing Date	3/16/2015
Incoming Investment	$500,000
Cap	**$3,500,000**
Discount to Series A	0%
Interest Rate	0%
Accrued Interest	$0
Total Convert	$500,000

Conversion Value

Pre-Money	Post-Money	$ Invested
$1,687,500	$1,357,143	$1,500,000

Appendix

7.7 Example: Cap Table with Existing Debt Notes *(continued)*

CONVERTIBLE NOTE (1)

Closing Date	3/16/2016
Incoming Investment	$500,000
Cap	
Discount to Series A	20%
Interest Rate	0%
Accrued Interest	$0
Total Convert	$500,000

Conversion Value

Pre-Money	*Post-Money*	*$ Invested*
$625,000	$625,000	$625,000

Appendix

7.7 Example: Cap Table with Existing Debt Notes *(continued)*

Series A Details	
Raise Amount	$1,500,000
Pre-Money Valuation	$8,000,000

Notes Conversion	
Pre-Money Method (1)	
Pre-Money	$8,000,000
Series A Investment	$1,500,000
Conversion Value	$2,312,500
Post-Money	$11,812,500
Post-Money Method (2)	
Pre-Money	$6,017,857
Series A Investment	$1,500,000
Conversion Value	$1,982,143
Post-Money	$9,500,000
$ Invested Method (3)	
Pre-Money	$8,000,000
Series A Investment	$1,500,000
Notes Amount	$1,000,000
Post-Money	$10,500,000

Appendix

7.7 Example: Cap Table with Existing Debt Notes *(continued)*

Share Price Calcs.

Case Toggle   3

Pre-Money	$8,000,000
Post-Money	$10,500,000
Series A Share Price	$6.88
Convertible Note 1 Share Price	$2.29
Convertible Note 2 Share Price	$5.50

Appendix

7.7 Example: Cap Table with Existing Debt Notes *(continued)*

Pro Forma Fully Diluted Cap Table	Common	Series A Preferred	Total	% FD
Founder 1	500,000		500,000	29%
Founder 2	500,000		500,000	29%
Convertible 1 noteholders		218,182	218,182	13%
Convertible 2 noteholders		90,909	90,909	5%
Series A		218,182	218,182	13%
Options	169,697		169,697	10%
	1,169,697	**527,273**	**1,696,970**	**100%**

Appendix

7.7 Example: Cap Table with Existing Debt Notes *(continued)*

Options Vesting Schedule

4-year cliff

Date	Vested Shares	% Vested	Unvested Shares	% Unvested
10/18/2019	0	0%		100%
10/17/2020	42,424	25%	127,273	75%
10/17/2021	84,848	50%	84,848	50%
10/17/2022	127,273	75%	42,424	25%
10/17/2023	**169,697**	**100%**	**0**	**0%**

Appendix

7.7 Example: Cap Table with Existing Debt Notes *(continued)*

Cap Table for Waterfall				
Liquidation Date			3/19/2021	
	Common	Series A Preferred	Total	% FD
Founder 1	500,000	0	500,000	32%
Founder 2	500,000	0	500,000	32%
Convertible 1 noteholders	0	218,182	218,182	14%
Convertible 2 noteholders	0	90,909	90,909	6%
Series A	0	218,182	218,182	14%
Options	42,424		42,424	3%
	1,042,424	**527,273**	**1,569,697**	**100%**

Appendix

7.8 Example: Statement of Operations[67]

Use the following as a reference of components you may need for your fund administration and accounting.

Venture Capital Fund, L.P.
Statement of Operations:
Year Ended Dec. 31, 20XX

Investment income	
Interest	4,087,000
Dividends	2,543,000
Other income	148,000
Total investment income	6,778,000
Expenses	
Interest expense	168,000
Management fee	7,588,000
Organization costs	323,000
Broken deal costs	1,380,000
Professional fees and other	593,000
Total expenses	10,052,000
Net investment income (loss)	(3,274,000)
Realized and unrealized gain (loss) on investment	
Net realized gain (loss) on investments	25,865,000
Net change unrealized appreciation/ depreciation	18,173,000
Net gain (loss) on investments	44,038,000
Net income (loss)	40,764,000

Appendix

7.9 Example: Statement of Changes in Partners' Capital[68]

Use the following as a reference of components you may need for your fund administration and accounting.

Venture Capital Fund, L.P.
Statement of Changes in Partners' Capital
Year Ended Dec. 31, 20XX

	General Partner	Limited Partners	Total
	$	$	$
Partners' capital, start of yr.	75,908,000	682,981,000	759,889,000
Capital contributions	274,000	24,774,000	25,048,000
Capital distributions	(473,000)	(36,988,000)	(37,461,000)
Transfer of capital	---	---	---
Syndication costs	---	---	---
Allocation of net income (loss)			
Pro rata allocation	447,000	32,242,000	32,689,000
Carry allocation to GP	8,075,000	---	8,075,000
Contingent loss reallocation	---	---	---
Contingent loss restoration	---	---	---
Allocation of net income (loss)	8,522,000	32,242,000	40,764,000
	$	$	$
Partners' capital, end of year	84,231,000	703,009,000	788,240,000

Appendix

7.10 Example: Statement of Cash Flows[69]

Use the following as a reference of components you may need for your fund administration and accounting.

Venture Capital Fund, L.P.
Statement of Cash Flows
Year Ended Dec. 31, 20XX

Cash flows from operating activities	$
Net income (loss)	40,764,000
Adjustments to reconcile net income (loss) to net cash provided by (used in) operating activities	
Net realized gain (loss) on investments	(25,865,000)
Net change in unrealized appreciation or depreciation on investments	(18,173,000)
Changes in operating assets and liabilities:	
Purchases of investments	(75,637,000)
Proceeds from sale of investments	84,175,000
Interest and dividends receivable	448,000
Due from related parties	(22,000)
Escrow proceeds receivable	455,000
Other assets	90,000
Management fee payable	173,000
Payable for investment purchase transactions	(41,500)
Due to related parties	(35,500)
Accrued expenses and other liabilities	87,000
Net cash provided by (used in) operating activities	6,418,000

Appendix

7.10 Example: Statement of Cash Flows *(continued)*

Cash flows from financing activities

Capital contributions, net of change in capital contributions receivable	24,100,000
Capital distributions, net of change in capital distributions payable	(37,363,000)
Proceeds from loans payable	2,055,000
Repayments of loans payable	(2,750,000)
Net cash provided by (used in) financing activities	(13,958,000)
Net change in cash and cash equivalents	(7,540,000)
Cash and cash equivalents, beginning of year	15,803,000
Cash and cash equivalents, end of year	$ 8,263,000

Supplemental disclosure of cash flow information

Cash paid during the year for interest	$ 140,000

Supplemental disclosure of non-cash information

Distribution of securities, at fair value (cost basis of $35,000)	$ 5,000,000

Appendix

7.11 Additional Reading

The following can be used as additional reading resources.

- **"GoingVC Venture Capital Fund Model," GoingVC Team**[70]
  - Guy, A., & Banerjee, V. (2020, April 2). GoingVC Venture Capital Fund Model. Retrieved from https://www.goingvc .com/goingvc-venture-capital-fund-model/
- **"How VC Funds Work — Structure Chart for Venture Capital Fund," The Venture Alley**[71]
  - Bearman, A. (2011, February 27). How VC Funds Work — Structure Chart for Venture Capital Fund (US Fund). Retrieved from https://www.theventurealley.com/2011/02 /how-vc-funds-work-typical-fund-structure/
- **"VC Funds 101: Understanding Venture Fund Structures, Team Compensation, Fund Metrics and Reporting," VCpreneur**[72]
  - Takatkah, A. (2019, April 16). VC Funds 101: Understanding Venture Fund Structures, Team Compensation, Fund Metrics and Reporting. Retrieved from https://vcpreneur.com/vc -funds-101-understanding-venture-fund-structures-team -compensation-fund-metrics-and-reporting-152b02e8504a

NOTES

Chapter 8
Portfolio Composition

Chapter 8
Portfolio Composition

Creating Value through Returns

In the last decade, the rise of Emerging Manager Venture Capital (EMVC) has leapt exponentially; the number of new venture funds has grown 245% over the past ten years, with 415 in 2010 and crossing 1,000 in 2020.[73] Additionally, the EMVC asset class is still growing and is expected to triple in the next ten years. Thus, masses of EMVC fund managers are experiencing a steep learning curve around how to launch and grow their funds. These fund managers are building businesses and looking to generate strong performance returns for their investor base.

Accurate reporting on the performance of your fund is a critical part of the investment process. With your fund administrator's help, you should track key performance metrics such as Internal Rate of Return (IRR), Multiple on Invested Capital (MOIC), Return on Investment (ROI), Distributions to Paid-in Capital (DPI), Residual Value to Paid-in Capital (RVPI), and Total Value to Paid-in-Capital (TVPI).

In this chapter, we will share how funds in the EMVC and MicroVC asset class are commonly composed and how they are performing. This information is not intended to be exhaustive or representative of the entire industry, as some regions and funds may not be featured here. Instead, this is a glimpse at the EMVC asset class and what trends might be applicable to your own returns and portfolio composition, including the number of portfolio companies, fund size, number of general partners, follow-ons, co-investments, and more. Use these components to create a baseline for your fund for internal tracking as well as investor conversations.

Defining Fund Managers

There are many definitions of EMVC that vary or have additional parameters. EMVC funds are generally a subset of Venture Capital firms that seek equity or equity-linked investments in privately held, high-growth startups and small to medium-sized enterprises with strong growth potential.[74]

When defining EMVC, some industry participants use the amount of assets under management (AUM), the number of funds, or even years of investing experience to describe the category. Industry norms commonly characterize an EMVC fund as sub $1bb-$2bb AUM, approximately $100mm to $250mm per fund, fewer than four funds, and a track record of five to ten years.[75] A common misconception is that EMVC encompasses only first-time fund managers, but there are a broad swath of fund managers, ranging across experience, variety, and investment focus.

In our expanded analysis of the EMVC space, we have also identified a category of Transitional EMVC (T-EMVC) that is able to compete at investing during the seed and early stages. These T-EMVCs generally represent an agile subset of the EMVC ecosystem as sub $250mm AUM, approximately $50mm to $100mm per fund, fewer than four funds, and non-traditional venture backgrounds, diverse intellects, alternative illustration of investment ability and long-term track record, and/or launching with sweat equity portfolios, fund "zeros," or foundry funds. Plus, T-EMVCs often have strong community, operator, or Founder networks.

Thus, T-EMVCs are not simply Micro Venture Capital (MicroVC; sub $100mm) or Nano Venture Capital (NanoVC; sub $25mm). Instead, they are a related subgroup of fund managers who are incredibly nimble, and, although T-EMVCs may fit into some categorizations of EMVC, MicroVC, and NanoVC, the following data should not be considered your only comparable sample set.

Industry Insights

The following outlines several highlights across the industry categories of EMVC, MicroVC, NanoVC, and the recently defined T-EMVC. The following highlights are based on industry data and interviews collected:

- Fund managers have shown how challenging and competitive surviving in the venture industry can be, given that, on average, it will take a first-time fund manager 12 to 18 months[76] or more to raise their fund, if it gets raised at all.
- We see 55% of fund managers operating as solo general partners (GPs) for Fund I and 36% bringing on another general partner when they reach Fund II.[77]
- Many note that solo GPs are now frequently competing to lead pre-seed, seed, Series A, and later-stage rounds against traditional venture capital firms. Often, their brand of the fund equals that of the individual. Solo GPs may also have close relationships with Founders that give the ability to write larger checks, for example, to invest more than $5mm in rounds, than super angels or funds with greater than $50mm in assets under management.[78]
- A vast majority of funds split investments between pre-seed at 30%, seed at 39%, and Series A at 19%. The remaining 12% is focused on investments in Series B, C, D, and more.[79]
- In general, once a fund manager begins deploying capital, they will invest in an average of 11 companies per fund.[80]
- Most fund managers raise an average of 1.2 funds; thus, they often do not go on to raise a second fund.[81]

Your Fund Components

While you construct your portfolio, keep in mind the following useful tips to give yourself an edge.

---

1. Investment Thesis

- What is your team's unfair competitive advantage? How will you understand/access/own companies better than others?
- How big is the sector/market of focus? Is the market growing or largely untapped?
- Can your model support top quartile returns?
- Is there an opportunity to scale?

---

2. Fund Model

- What stage of companies are you investing in? For example: pre-seed, seed, Series A/B, early-stage, late-stage, growth
- What sectors, geographies, and classifications are you investing in? For example: B2B, consumer, hardware, deep tech, generalist, impact
- What check sizes are you writing? Any maximum allocations by sector?
- What is the size of your fund?
- How many deals have you done in the last year?
- What is your deployment timeline? For example: two years, three years, four years
- What is your ROI timeline?
- Do you hold capital reserves? How much?

3. Deals / Sourcing

- How are your deals sourced? How are they tracked?
- Do you exhibit nimble access to deals?
- What best-in-class networks do you leverage, if any?
- How are investment decisions made? Who and how many people are involved? Who has final say? Do you have an investment committee?
- What resources do you provide to their portfolio companies beyond capital?
- Do you participate in opportunistic deals?

4. Ownership / Pro Rata

- Do you have pro rata ownership rights, which are the right, but not the obligation, to invest in future funding rounds? What percentage?
- Are you valuation-sensitive for deals? Do you have a valuation range? How so?
- How will you handle special purpose vehicles (SPVs)? Have you done them previously?
- How do you coalesce other investors for SPVs? Do any other specific investors have priority in SPVs?

5. Performance

- Do you have an alternative demonstration of investment ability, if a "conventional" track record is not available? For example, a non-traditional investing background, prior

angel investments, previous operator knowledge, a foundry fund, an advisory share portfolio, a fund zero?
- How do you illustrate diversity of intellect?
- Are you able to mitigate the influence of "group think"?

6. Case Studies
- How did you get into the case study deal? What was the source?
- Date invested/involved? Ownership?
- Why did you participate?
- Are you planning to invest again in the next round?
- What are the next milestones?
- Any top quality co-investors?

7. Structure
- What is your fee structure? Management fee? Carry fee?
- What are fees on additional deals, such as SPVs?
- What is your capital call schedule?

8. Team
- Who is on your team? What are your backgrounds?
- Number of founding members or general partners? Tenure together? What is the split percentage of ownership across your team?
- How many employees other than GPs will you have?
- Who is a part of your leadership?
- What is your talent for finding compelling companies? Do you often access stellar deals?

- What are your interpersonal dynamics?

9. Purpose
- Is your team planning for longevity? Or does your firm cease to exist if the founding team leaves?
- Do you have an overlooked protagonist with a significant stake? Does your team have a woman, person of color, LGBTQ+, or military veteran leader?
- Is your team coachable? Forthcoming with information? Any red flags or obnoxious behavior of concern?
- How often will you update investors on performance?
- Is your team doing something truly unique?

10. Investors
- What types of investors will you have?
- How many investors will you have?

As you consider your portfolio composition, be sure to understand how and why your portfolio was constructed and how it has evolved. Understanding why your portfolio is composed in a specific manner will also help you answer questions from investors about your fund.

Scan this QR code

or visit
https://www.venturefundblueprint.com/blueprints/
portfoliocomposition

to see the interactive workbook and learn more about
The Venture Fund Blueprint

Appendix

8.1 Fund Manager Data: Number of Portfolio Companies[82]

The following can be used as industry data points that highlight the number of portfolio companies invested in for fund managers.

Number of Unique Portfolio Companies

Fund Size in Millions	$0mm to $5mm	$5mm to $15mm	$15mm to 50mm	$50mm to $100mm	Overall $0mm to $100mm
Average Number of Unique Portfolio Companies	12.8	19.2	20.3	25.3	19.5
Median Number of Unique Portfolio Companies	8	9	12.5	15	11
Number of Funds in Sample Size	36	28	44	23	113

Sources and General Methodological Notes:

Data Set: Funds raised by US investment firms in Crunchbase's "Venture Capital," "Micro VC," and "Accelerator" categories. We only included firms founded in or after 2008. When categorizing a list of fund names into fund numbers (e.g., "Acme Ventures Fund II, LP" would be classified as "Fund II") we were sure to include only primary/flagship funds. Sidecar funds, one-off special situations funds, opportunity funds, and so on, were labeled as such when legal entity names made clear what the nature of the fund was.

Appendix

8.1 Fund Manager Data: Number of Portfolio Companies
(continued)

Methodology: We selected Fund I's raised by firms with only one fund listed on their Crunchbase profile. Crunchbase data discloses the firms that invested in a round, but does not typically specify the specific fund that was the source of capital for the deal.

Appendix

8.2 Fund Manager Data: Fund Size[83]

The following can be used as industry data points that highlight fund sizes for fund managers.

Fund I versus Fund II

For Fund I's between $0mm and $5mm

	Fund I	Fund II
Number of Firms in Sample Size	74	
Number of Funds in Sample Size	74	43
Average Fund Size	$2.63mm	$15mm
Median Fund Size	$2.5mm	$11mm
Average Percentage Growth/Shrinkage		485%
Median Percentage Growth/Shrinkage		200%
Count of Fund IIs Larger than Fund I		40
Count of Fund IIs Smaller than Fund I		3
Count of Fund IIs Equally Sized to Fund I		0

Appendix

8.2 Fund Manager Data: Fund Size *(continued)*

For Fund I's between $5mm and $15mm

	Fund I	Fund II
Number of Firms in Sample Size	79	
Number of Funds in Sample Size	79	44
Average Fund Size	$9.95mm	$31.2mm
Median Fund Size	$10mm	$31mm
Average Percentage Growth/Shrinkage		244%
Median Percentage Growth/Shrinkage		202%
Count of Fund IIs Larger than Fund I		40
Count of Fund IIs Smaller than Fund I		3
Count of Fund IIs Equally Sized to Fund I		1

Appendix

8.2 Fund Manager Data: Fund Size *(continued)*

For Fund I's between $15mm and $50mm

	Fund I	Fund II
Number of Firms in Sample Size	160	
Number of Funds in Sample Size	160	101
Average Fund Size	$30.5mm	$63.8mm
Median Fund Size	$28.5mm	$51.3mm
Average Percentage Growth/Shrinkage		112.5%
Median Percentage Growth/Shrinkage		81.7%
Count of Fund IIs Larger than Fund I		93
Count of Fund IIs Smaller than Fund I		7
Count of Fund IIs Equally Sized to Fund I		1

Appendix

8.2 Fund Manager Data: Fund Size *(continued)*

For Fund I's between $50mm and $100mm

	Fund I	Fund II
Number of Firms in Sample Size	78	
Number of Funds in Sample Size	78	45
Average Fund Size	$79.5mm	$155.6mm
Median Fund Size	$80mm	$125mm
Average Percentage Growth/Shrinkage		87.5%
Median Percentage Growth/Shrinkage		73%
Count of Fund IIs Larger than Fund I		39

Sources and General Methodological Notes:

Data Set: Funds raised by US investment firms in Crunchbase's "Venture Capital," "Micro VC," and "Accelerator" categories. We only included firms founded in or after 2008. When categorizing a list of fund names into fund numbers (e.g., "Acme Ventures Fund II, LP" would be classified as "Fund II") we were sure to include only primary/flagship funds. Sidecar funds, one-off special situations funds, opportunity funds, and so on, were labeled as such when legal entity names made it clear what the nature of the fund was.

Methodology: We selected Fund I's raised by firms with only one fund listed on their Crunchbase profile. Crunchbase data discloses the firms that invested in a round, but does not typically specify the specific fund which was the source of capital for the deal.

Appendix

8.3 Fund Manager Data: Number of General Partners [84]

The following can be used as industry data points that highlight the number of general partners for fund managers.

Number of General Partners

Fund Size in Millions ($)	$0mm to $5mm	$5mm to $15mm	$15mm to $50mm	$50mm to $100mm	Overall $0mm to $100mm
Total Number of Funds in Sample Size	44	59	98	54	**255**
Number of Solo-GP Funds	27	28	64	29	**148**
Number of Funds with 2 GPs	12	24	21	19	**76**
Number of Funds with 3 GPs	1	6	11	1	**19**
Number of Funds with 4+ GPs	4	1	2	5	**12**

Appendix

8.3 Fund Manager Data: Number of General Partners *(continued)*

Sources and General Methodological Notes:

Methodology: From the People table in Crunchbase, we created an unduplicated list of individuals holding a job title containing one of the following strings: "founding partner," "general partner," "managing partner," "managing director," "founding general partner," or "co-founding partner" (case-insensitive). We merged this table with the enriched funds table, on the UUID (a 32-character alphanumeric globally-unique identifier of a Node across the entire CrunchBase Graph) of the venture firm. We then filtered down to a relatively narrow set: Fund I's raised by firms with only one fund on record. We did this to avoid conflating numbers from firms with more than one fund raised, which may have added additional partners to their roster subsequent to raising the first fund.

Appendix

8.4 Fund Manager Data: Distribution in Size of New Venture Funds[85]

The following can be used as industry data points that highlight the sizes of new venture funds.

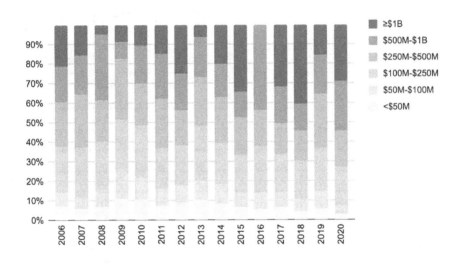

	2006	2007	2008	2009	2010	2011	2012	2013	2014	2015	2016	2017	2018	2019	2020
<$50M	$3.2	$3.2	$3.5	$2.9	$3.8	$3.8	$4.1	$3.8	$4.7	$5.1	$4.6	$6.0	$5.6	$5.3	$3.1
$50M - $100M	$3.3	$3.0	$4.5	$4.0	$3.9	$4.1	$4.2	$3.8	$5.6	$6.4	$8.1	$7.6	$7.8	$8.6	$5.5
$100M - $250M	$10.4	$13.9	$12.5	$6.6	$9.6	$10.2	$9.2	$10.5	$12.0	$15.5	$20.8	$18.4	$24.1	$20.3	$21.6
$250M - $500M	$10.3	$14.9	$10.8	$8.0	$7.5	$12.4	$8.4	$9.3	$13.3	$15.8	$16.7	$15.0	$19.5	$25.5	$20.7
$500M - $1B	$8.3	$10.8	$17.1	$2.4	$6.9	$11.2	$8.3	$7.7	$9.7	$10.7	$22.2	$17.6	$16.9	$18.6	$28.3
≥$1B	$9.5	$8.5	$2.5	$2.2	$3.8	$7.3	$11.6	$2.4	$11.4	$27.9	$16.5	$30.2	$50.7	$14.4	$32.4

Appendix

8.5 Example: Portfolio Model/Base Model[86]

The following is an example of a portfolio model. Use this to help model the companies in your own fund.

Follow-On Reserves

#	Name	Total Invested ($mm)	Follow-On Complete	Expected Follow-On ($mm)	Total Expected Invested ($mm)	Pre-Money Val. ($mm)
Follow-On Complete?		Sum $1.4		Sum $0.23	Sum $1.67	Sum $4.00
1	Conecom	$0.25		$0.03	$0.28	$0.00
2	Scotfind	$0.25		$0.03	$0.28	$0.00
3	Massive	$0.20		$0.03	$0.23	$4.00
4	BetaTech	$0.20		$0.03	$0.23	$0.00
5	Initech	$0.30		$0.10	$0.40	$0.00
6	Sterling Cooper	$0.25		$0.03	$0.28	$0.00
Follow-On Complete?		Sum $1.8		Sum $0.05	Sum $1.85	Sum $10.00
7	Zotware	$0.30	✓	$0.03	$0.33	$10.00
8	Streethex	$0.70	✓	$0.00	$0.70	$0.00
9	Hooli	$0.40	✓	$0.00	$0.40	$0.00
10	Globex	$0.40	✓	$0.03	$0.43	$0.00
		Sum $3.2		Sum $0.28	Sum $3.52	Sum $14.00

Appendix

8.6 Example: Portfolio Model/Base Model of Financial Investments [87]

The following is an example of a portfolio model. Use this to help model the companies in your own fund.

Financial Investments

#	Name	Funding Rounds	Total Invested ($mm)	Pre-Money Val. ($mm)	Total Company Owner-ship	Total Company Shares Out-standing	Total Company Shares Owned	Portfolio Founders
1	Initech	Initech (Pre-Seed)	$0.30	$0.00	NaN	0	0	Renee Wickline
2	Massive DB	Massive (Seed)	$0.20	$4.00	3.17%	7,892,345	250,000	Marylouise Kittinger
3	Conecom	Conecom (Pre-Seed)	$0.25	$0.00	NaN	0	0	Cleta Gesell
4	Zotware	Zotware (Seed) Zotware (Pre-Seed)	$0.30	$10.00	1.76%	19,872,342	350,000	Ward Orear
5	Streethex	Streethex (Seed) Streethex (Pre-Seed)	$0.70	$0.00	NaN	0	0	Vina Bloodworth
6	Hooli	Hooli (Pre-Seed) Hooli (Pre-Seed)	$0.40	$0.00	NaN	0	0	Alfreda Nye
7	Sterling Cooper	Sterling Cooper (Pre-Seed)	$0.25	$0.00	NaN	0	0	Brit Bohlen
8	Globex	Globex (Seed) Globex (Pre-Seed)	$0.40	$0.00	NaN	0	0	Lurlone Herdon
9	Scotfind	Scotfind (Pre-Seed)	$0.25	$0.00	NaN	0	0	Ruthie Tilghman
10	Betatech	Betatech (Pre-Seed)	$0.20	$0.00	NaN	0	0	Joshua Test
			Sum $3.25	Sum $14.00	Sum NaN	Sum 2,7764,687	Sum 600,000	

Appendix

8.7 Example: Portfolio Multiple[88]

The following model shows that investing in more than 100 companies at the earliest stages does, in fact, reduce the risk of losing investors' money and may very well lead to investing in an outlier. A portfolio comprising 100 companies has a theoretical 99% chance of returning the capital and a 57% chance of achieving a 2x return — nearly twice the likelihood of a portfolio of only 10 startups.

% of Portfolios that Equal or Exceed Multiple

Port Size	1x	2x	3x	4x	5x
10	68%	29%	17%	12%	9%
20	80%	34%	19%	13%	9%
30	88%	41%	23%	15%	11%
50	95%	47%	25%	16%	11%
100	99%	57%	30%	17%	13%
500	99.9%	86%	43%	24%	17%
1,000	99.9%	95%	52%	28%	18%

Appendix

8.8 Example: Investments per Round[89]

The following table shows just how much investment strategy and overall portfolio construction can differ between fund managers, with some investing in over 100 companies and others in under 10. Also, the data shows that most fund managers — the first three quartiles — invest in fewer than 30 companies. This can be seen as a signal that most fund managers perceive 30 as the number of investments above which it becomes increasingly difficult to properly assess and select deals and/or effectively support the portfolio companies.

Investments Per Round

	Initial Round	1st Follow-on	2nd Follow-on
Average	27	15	8
Median	22	13	7
Maximum	133	75	22
Top Quartile	29	17	10
Bottom Quartile	18	10	5
Minimum	8	4	0

Appendix

8.9 Example: Ownership Percentage[90]

Another very important aspect of portfolio construction relates to fund managers' ownership stakes in each portfolio company, as this will ultimately be key to the impact each outlier will have on the fund's returns.

Ownership (%)

	Initial Round	At Exit
Average	12.44	10.12
Median	11.10	10.00
Maximum	25.00	30.00
Top Quartile	17.50	15.00
Bottom Quartile	9.27	6.35
Minimum	2.00	2.50

Appendix

8.10 Exercise: Portfolio Investments Summary

Use the following table to summarize your fund's portfolio investments.

Company	Date of Initial Investment	Amount Invested	Current Value	Ownership	Board Seat	Business Summary
\<alpha order\>	\<date\>	\<$$\>	\<$$\>	\<%\>	\<Y/N\>	\<one-line summary\>

NOTES

Chapter 9
Legal

Chapter 9
Legal

Establishing Your Legal Framework

Setting up the proper legal structure of your fund before launch is critical to success in the long term. Fund managers enlist legal counsel to help lead your fund's formation while providing guidance along the way.

Your legal team will help balance the competing interests of your limited partners, general partners, and employees. As you launch your fund, your counsel will work with you to design the optimal Limited Partnership Agreement (LPA), facilitate negotiations with prospective limited partners, and manage the closing process for your fundraise.

Fund managers typically use separate law firms for investment term sheets, contracts, employment matters, and more. This could be for cost-saving measures or because they wish to delegate work based on a firm's specific expertise.

In this chapter, we will discuss some of the main ways you will work with your legal team as well as the legal components to consider when launching your fund.

Structure[91]

Although variations of legal setup are specific to each fund manager, the following will expand on common relationships that exist.

Your fund structure is generally determined by the relationship between your management company Limited Liability Company (LLC), management company General Partner (GP), and Limited Partner (LP) entities.

The management company LLC is typically formed where the fund manager's business will geographically and legally operate, for example, in California. It is important to note that this is the entity that faces the SEC. The management company provides operational services to each fund.

The management company GP entity is responsible for the management, profits, and, most importantly, the liability for debts.

In a Limited Partnership, investors commit capital to the fund and hold equity as LPs.

With the help of your legal counsel, the legal agreement of the management company GP will be formed under an LPA governing document. The LPA is the agreement that your LP investors will be subject to. An LPA defines the terms of your partnership and helps protect the interests of your success and your future business.

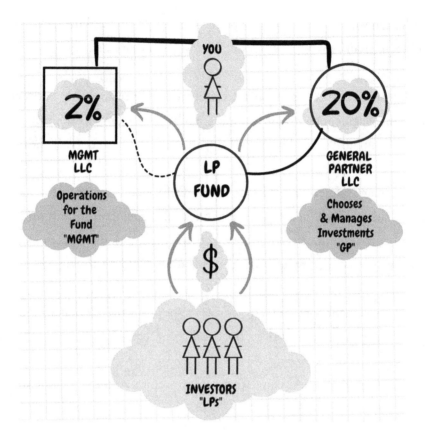

Expanded Definitions

Limited Liability Company (LLC) and Management Company

Typically, the management company is formed as an LLC where the fund manager's business will geographically and legally operate, for example, in California. It is important to note that this is the entity that faces the SEC. The management company provides the operational services to each fund. The management company receives the management fee from the fund and uses it to pay management company expenses related to operating the firm, such as salaries, rent for office space, and equipment.

General Partner (GP)

The management company GP is the entity that acts as the decision maker for the fund and also receives the carry paid by the fund. The GP is typically formed as a Delaware LLC in the US. Usually, successor funds will have a new GP to facilitate potentially different carry allocations. Note that the GP may also be an LP if your state has advantageous tax reasons to structure the fund as such. Be sure to consult your tax advisor for further details.

Limited Partner (LP)

A fund is most often formed as an LP entity, where the investors commit capital to the fund and hold equity interests as limited partners. Depending upon the size and vintage of your fund, the investors that make up the LP can be individuals or entities, for example, high net worth individuals, institutions, family offices, fund-of-funds, endowments, foundations, universities, or public and private pension plans. Typically, each of your LPs will also need to be "qualified purchasers": a person or business holding an investment portfolio with a value of $5 million or more. Normally the fund elects to be treated as a partnership for tax purposes to allow for pass-through tax treatment rather than two layers of taxation of profits of the fund. Be sure to consult your tax advisor for further details.

General Partner and Limited Partner Nomenclature

In somewhat deceptive nomenclature, the individual owner and operator of your fund may also be referred to as a fund GP or managing member. A fund may have more than one fund GP making investment decisions.

Before adding another fund GP to your fund, it is critical to ensure that you are comfortable with the team dynamics, for example, the number of years you have known each other, how well you know each other, whether you share common values and integrity, how similar your business practices are, whether you have invested together, and your collective process to make decisions.

The terms *Limited Partner* and LP may also be used to describe the individual investors who committed capital to your fund — in addition to the limited partnership entity where the investors commit capital to the fund, as previously described.

Agreements[93]

Operating Agreement

The Operating Agreement (OA) is a legal document that outlines the ownership and member duties of your LLC. Typically, the managers of a general partnership are individuals referred to as "fund managers," "managers," "managing members," or "a board of managers." In some cases, however, the general partner may be managed by another entity.

Limited Partner Advisory Committee

Your Limited Partner Advisory Committee (LPAC) is the governing body consisting of select LPs who oversee your fund. Your LPAC will have certain obligations and capabilities that are specified in the LPA, including but not limited to addressing conflicts of interest, valuation methodology, and consents or approvals pre-defined in your governing documents.

Standard Terms

Using standard terms in your LPA can generally help alleviate friction and bring about the fastest execution of your fund formation. It is standard for your fund to pay an annual management fee to the fund's management company based on a percentage of the capital commitments in the fund. This management fee is used to pay management expenses and salaries. Standard management fees are usually 2%. In addition, as a fund manager you will usually keep a percentage of the fund's profits, known as carried interest or "carry." Standard carry fees are 20%; however, some funds take up to 30% based on their specialty and track record. Using a standard management fee and carry fee in your LPA can aid in the seamless setup of your formation documents.

Negotiable Terms

Negotiable terms include case-by-case matters that will depend on the size and operations of your fund. These may include capital distribution timing, capital call obligations for LPs, co-investor rights, percentages due upon closing, notice periods, investment periods, the term of the fund, and general partner commitments. Be mindful that GP capital commitments may have some common requirements, for example, 1 to 2% of the fund, cumulative or per GP. GP commitments may also have some nuanced structures, such as a payment from the LLC to LP after capital contributions, a GP loan from the LLC to the GP to pay out of carry, or promissory notes.

Common Restrictions

Some common investment restrictions may include limitations on the number of deals in a period of time, limitations to not recycle more than a certain percentage of capital such as 20% of the fund, limitations on single deals, limitations to have under 100 limited partners in your fund, limitations in how much leverage you can have under the venture capital exemption, tax restrictions on holding capital at year-end and clear balances on December 31st, and suspension of business if a key person in the LPA leaves the fund.

Non-Standard Terms

Non-standard terms are rare and generally not advisable unless there are extenuating circumstances, such as if LPs have side agreements or rights, if your fund prohibits certain distributions, or if your LPs are permitted to opt out of certain investments.

Best Practices with Legal Counsel[94]

Communication

While fundraising or going through different periods of growth for your fund, it is advisable to keep constant communications with your legal counsel. Your legal counsel will help guide you through appropriate timing for your fundraising round close, assist in managing negotiations with prospective limited partners, and review exceptions to your formation documents with LPs.

State, Federal, and Regulatory Registrations/Filings

Be sure to coordinate with your legal counsel around regulatory filings including state and federal registrations, such as registrations in Delaware, registrations in your home state, securities filings with the Securities and Exchange Commission (SEC) and states, annual filings, and disclosure documents. In addition, unless an exemption is available (discussed further below), your management company may be required to become registered as an investment adviser with the state securities commission or the Financial Industry Regulatory Authority (FINRA). These registrations may also require periodic payments, where you may need to process transfers by coordinating with your fund administrator, if you have hired one, or with your own finance team by tracking these tasks on an ongoing basis and creating calendar reminders.

Ongoing Legal Matters

Be sure to inform your legal counsel of any disruptions with investors meeting capital calls or from abiding by the rules and timing set forth in your governing documents. Make your legal counsel aware of pending lawsuits that arise with your portfolio companies, including employee disputes that may affect the fund or its returns or broader lawsuits that may impact the fund reputationally.

Legal for Portfolio Company Deals

Diligence

Before deciding to enter into an investment, it is important to establish a process for conducting diligence on each company, from research until funding. Many fund managers will create a formal method by which prospective companies move through their pipeline of due diligence to make the process a good experience for the founders. Keep in mind that conducting company diligence can be a significant time commitment.

Be sure to share your portfolio company diligence with your legal counsel to provide them with the details needed to prepare your deal documents. Some diligence you may wish to collect ahead of passing on to your legal counsel could include the company's articles of incorporations, fundraising history, documents from past fundraising rounds, previous side letters, and their Board of Directors structure. In addition, include background on their financial spending, cash on hand, outstanding lawsuits if applicable, outstanding debt, employee agreements, and any intellectual property.

Preparation of Deal Documents

Your legal counsel for deals, who may or may not be the same as your legal counsel for fund formation, can work with your portfolio companies to execute deal documents. Some of the major considerations around deal documentation include understanding which protections to put in place for dilution and future rounds and side letters that determine governance, board seats, follow-on minimums, and information rights. Be sure to work with your legal counsel for deals to verify each portfolio company's formation documents and their corporate governance requirements.

Once your legal counsel is ready to prepare deal documents, they can help you understand if your investment expectations are being met with those deal documents. Your legal counsel should be heavily involved in helping you to understand the legal and structural matters of the investment. Most often, fund managers will request legal counsel's assistance to understand their ownership of the portfolio company. When entering into a pre-seed or seed investment, your fund may execute a note or a Simple Agreement for Future Equity (SAFE) on the portfolio company, which is generally a standard document. Later, when participating in Series A deals and beyond, your fund may instead execute a term sheet, which is commonly used for priced rounds where investors are purchasing newly issued stock in the company at an agreed-upon price per share, to outline the conditions under which an investment will be made.

Deal Valuations

When signing deal terms, be cognizant of pre-money and post-money valuations that respectively represent the company's estimated worth before and after investor capital injections, the current list of cap table investors, and the total round size. If you are entering a priced round, where investors are purchasing newly issued stock in the company at an agreed-upon price per share, and are not a lead fund manager, your legal counsel can help you to assess your ongoing rights, such as pro rata rights, which are the right, but not the obligation, to invest in those future funding rounds. If you are leading a round, your legal counsel will play a much larger role to help you complete the priced round documentation and convert the existing debt or note, which is the exchange of the debt for equity when a future equity round is raised. With a SAFE note or other note, your legal counsel can help you understand how much equity to expect in the portfolio company after the round is completed. It is important to highlight, however, that if you have executed an uncapped note, you may not know your percentage ownership of the portfolio company, which is considered uncommon and can be risky for some fund managers, as there is no guarantee of how much equity your money purchases.

Board of Directors Service

It is common for fund managers to seek a Board seat with the portfolio companies in which they invest. Your legal counsel can help you to document your intentions to secure a Board seat. Getting a Board seat is often a function of your relationship with the portfolio company. Being a member of the Board can be an important part of your role as a portfolio manager, not only for providing oversight but also for establishing a level of formality with the company CEO running the business. Be aware that if you are sitting on a Board, you will have fiduciary duties to the company and its other shareholders, as well as the potential for litigation and liability in that role.

Securities Laws[95]

Having a high-level practical overview of securities laws governed by the SEC is an important component of understanding your relationship with investors and stakeholders. Venture funds are subject to examination by the SEC and FINRA and subject to the same basic regulations as other forms of private securities investments.

Communication

Given that federal and state securities laws apply, you should be particularly careful about stating future projections or past performance with your investors. Be clear about communicating investment risks and do not overstate them. State and federal securities law requirements also restrict how and to whom you may offer fund interests; ensure that you discuss your investor base and fundraising plans with counsel ahead of time. Review the content and timing of your online presence with your legal counsel before making it available publicly so you do not run afoul of securities laws, including marketing limitations or regulations.

SEC Federal Laws

Although there are several relevant regulatory guidelines for fund managers, the following are some of the prominent securities laws to be mindful of, including the Investment Advisers Act of 1940, which deals generally with persons providing money management advice, and the Investment Company Act of 1940, which deals generally with pooled investment vehicles whose shares are available for purchase by the public.[96] In both cases, fund managers may elect for exemptions that remove some or all of their registration requirements. Be sure to consult your legal counsel for further details.

Investment Advisers Act of 1940 (Advisers Act)[97]

The Advisers Act regulates sole practitioners or firms, "advisers," that are engaged in the business of providing investment management services, investment advice, analysis, or reports regarding securities. Fund managers are subject to registration and regulation under the Advisers Act or state investment adviser laws, unless exempt. As such, determine with your legal counsel whether you will (a) operate as an investment adviser and be subject to registration and regulation under federal or state law, or (b) operate within an exemption. If you plan to become registered as an investment adviser, you will need to understand and conform to the licensing, disclosure, reporting, recordkeeping, custody, audit, compliance program, and other requirements that will apply to your business. If you plan to operate within an exemption, it is important to remember that state and federal securities disclosures will still apply to your business, along with anti-fraud laws.

There are various Advisers Act exemptions available to some of the following categories: (a) investment advisers to venture funds, if the portfolio and operations of the fund conform to an SEC rule defining venture funds[98] and small business investment companies (SBICs);[99] and (b) investment advisers working solely with private investment funds with aggregate assets under management of $150 million or less, provided the private funds all rely on Section 3(c)(1) or 3(c)(7) for an exemption from the Investment Company Act of 1940.[100]

Venture firms that rely on some of these exemptions must file and report as "exempt reporting advisers" with the SEC. Work with your legal counsel to ensure you are properly registered with the SEC and/or exempt.[101]

Investment Company Act of 1940 (1940 Act)[102]

The 1940 Act regulates investment companies. The 1940 Act defines an "investment company" as an issuer of securities to investors that engages primarily in investing, reinvesting, and trading of securities. The purpose of the 1940 Act is to regulate the operations, capital structure, leverage, asset valuation, liquidity requirements, corporation governance, securities offerings, reporting, and disclosures of investment companies, along with mutual funds, closed end funds, and exchange-traded funds.

Venture funds usually choose to rely on exclusions from the definition of an "investment company" provided by Sections 3(c)(1) and 3(c)(7) of the 1940 Act, the private fund exemptions.

A qualifying venture capital fund shall be excluded from the definition of an investment company provided it meets the following criteria:

Exclusions
- The fund is owned exclusively by high net worth and institutional "qualified purchasers"
- The fund is a "venture capital fund" as that term is defined for the "venture capital fund adviser" exemption under the Advisers Act
- The fund does not make a public offering of its securities[103]
- The fund must have no more than 250 beneficial owners. Congress recently broadened the 3(c)(1) private fund exemption to allow a "qualifying venture capital fund" to have up to 250 beneficial owners of its securities, rather than 100 or fewer beneficial owners. With respect to the 250 beneficial owners

limit, this is the exemption used for venture funds with no more than $10 million of capital commitments and uncalled committed capital. Note that a fund with 100 persons and 3(c)(1) can raise infinite money, while qualified purchaser and 3(c)(7) funds have no person limit under the 1940 Act.

A venture fund that does not meet these additional requirements for a "qualifying venture capital fund" may still rely on the traditional exclusion. Be aware that under its "integration" doctrine, the SEC may take the position that two or more funds under the same fund manager may be counted together as one large fund to determine whether you have fewer than 250 or 100 beneficial owners.

It is important to use a methodical approach to understand the legalities of becoming a fund manager and the significance of structuring your fund. Dedicate time to understand the full range of formation matters for your firm in order to have the best chance of a successful, seamless setup.

Scan this QR code

or visit

https://www.venturefundblueprint.com/blueprints/legal

to see the interactive workbook and learn more about
The Venture Fund Blueprint

Appendix

9.1 Example: Venture Fund Structure — VC Funds 101: Understanding Venture Fund Structures, Team Compensation, Fund Metrics and Reporting[104]

Refer to the following example structure to help you better understand your own fund.

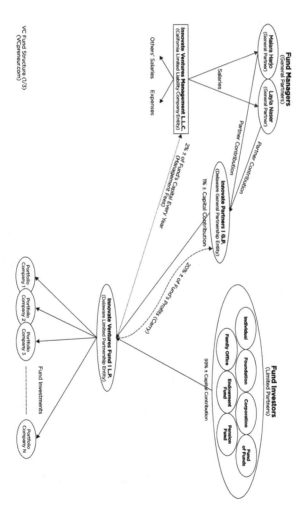

Appendix

9.2 Additional Securities Laws [105]

The following are additional securities laws you may wish to be familiar with.

Private Offerings of Securities, Section 4(a)(2) of the 1933 Act and Regulation D

Private funds and venture funds generally must be offered in private placements conducted under Section 4(a)(2) of the Securities Act of 1933 (1933 Act)[106] and Rule 506 of Regulation D under that section.[107] Regulation D is an SEC regulation that implements the private placement exemption. Regulation D offerings are advantageous to private companies or entrepreneurs that meet the requirements because funding can be obtained faster and at a lower cost than with a public offering. The private fund and venture fund exemptions require the fund to only issue its securities in private placements. Rule 506 of Regulation D is the simplest private placement exemption for private funds to use. The regulation allows capital to be raised through the sale of equity or debt securities without the need to register those securities with the SEC or state laws. Anti-fraud requirements apply to private placements.

Rule 506 of Regulation D

Rule 506 of Regulation D provides two distinct exemptions from registration for companies when they offer and sell securities. Companies relying on the Rule 506 exemptions can raise an unlimited amount of money and offer to an unlimited number of "accredited investors." Companies that comply with the requirements of Rule 506(b) or (c) do not have to register their offering of securities with the SEC, but they must file what is known as "Form D" electronically with the SEC after they first sell their securities. Form D is a brief notice that includes the names and addresses of the company's promoters, executive officers, and directors, and some details about the offering, but contains little other information about the company. Form D also requires disclosure of the 1940 Act exemption upon which a fund issuer relies. Rule 506(b) is by far the more favored exemption for offerings by private investment funds.

- Under Rule 506(b), a "safe harbor" under Section 4(a)(2) of the Securities Act, a company can be assured it is within the Section 4(a)(2) exemption by satisfying certain requirements, including the following:
  - The company cannot use "general solicitation" or advertising to market the securities.
  - The company may sell its securities to an unlimited number of "accredited investors" and up to 35 non-accredited purchasers. All non-accredited investors, either alone or with a purchaser representative, must be sophisticated — that is, they must have sufficient knowledge and experience in financial and business matters to make them capable of evaluating the merits and risks of the prospective investment and must receive disclosures analogous to those provided in a public offering of securities. Private funds generally do not offer securities to non-accredited investors, with occasional exceptions for family members and close friends of the managers.
  - The issuer, its predecessors and related persons and affiliates, the investment manager, and any placement agent or solicitor

for the issuer must not have been previously found by a court or agency to have engaged in various kinds of disqualifying offenses.

- Under Rule 506(b), an issuer is allowed to reasonably rely on written representations of investors that they are "accredited investors."

- The SEC interprets the Rule 506(b) prohibition on "general solicitation" to restrict the offer and sale of securities solely to investors with which the issuer, its personnel, or a placement agent have a substantial preexisting business relationship that predates the offering.

- Companies must disclose material information to investors about the fund and its securities and not violate the antifraud prohibitions of the securities laws. Any information a company provides to investors must be free from false or misleading statements. A fund should not exclude any information if the omission makes what is provided to investors false or misleading. Companies must give non-accredited investors disclosure documents that are generally the same as those used in Regulation A or registered offerings, including financial statements, which in some cases may need to be certified or audited by an accountant. If a company provides information to accredited investors, it must make this information available to non-accredited investors as well.

- The securities must be restricted as to transfer.

- The company must be available to answer questions by prospective purchasers.

- Under Rule 506(c), a company can broadly solicit and generally advertise the offering and still be deemed to be in compliance with the exemption's requirements if:
  - The investors in the offering are all accredited investors; and
  - The company takes reasonable steps to verify that the investors are accredited investors, which could include reviewing documentation, such as W-2s, tax returns, bank and brokerage statements, credit reports and the like.
  - Due to the reluctance of investors to provide this documentation, the extra work required of the issuer, and the risks to a private fund under this exemption, few private investment funds rely on Rule 506(c).

Blue Sky Laws

Blue sky laws are state-level anti-fraud regulations that require issuers of securities to be registered and to disclose details of their offerings.[108] These laws are designed to protect investors against fraudulent sales practices and activities.[109] An offering conducted under Rule 506 preempts conflicting state private offering exemptions, but the issuer must file Form D with the relevant states and pay a fee, generally within a short period after the first sale in each state. For an on-going fund offering, Form D is updated annually with the SEC and relevant states.

Business Development Companies and Small Business Investment Companies

Business development companies (BDCs) and small business investment companies (SBICs) may become more relevant to your venture capital firm as you begin to expand. A BDC is a type of closed-end fund registered with the SEC that makes investments in developing and financially distressed firms. Some, if not all, of the 1940 Act applies to BDCs. Many BDCs issue shares that are publicly traded and are open to retail investors. BDCs offer investors high-dividend yields and some capital appreciation potential. BDCs can be structured to provide pass-through tax treatment similar to a mutual fund, which is otherwise unavailable for publicly traded companies.

An SBIC is a type of privately owned investment company that is licensed by the Small Business Administration (SBA). Small business investment companies supply small businesses with financing in both the equity and debt arenas. They are a viable alternative form of organization used by venture capital firms to supply capital to small enterprises. SBA guarantees are available for debt securities issued by an SBA, which allows an SBIC to leverage up its portfolio on favorable terms.

Volcker Rule

The Volcker Rule was adopted as part of the 2010 Dodd-Frank Act to prohibit banks that accept FDIC-insured deposits from owning interests as principal in private funds, which are defined in that rule as "covered funds." There are several exceptions to this prohibition, including exemptions for BDC and SBICs. The federal financial regulators have proposed an additional exemption for venture capital funds and credit funds. The proposal aims to broaden the categories of private funds in which banks can invest. The proposed exemption, if adopted, would also allow banking organizations to engage in a greater degree of "parallel investment" alongside covered funds. Be sure to consult your legal counsel for further details if you are interested in attracting banking organizations as investors in your planned venture capital fund.

Regarding disclosure requirements and anti-fraud liability, there is not a specific SEC form or set of disclosures required for private offerings. Private funds and private offerings are subject to disclosure obligations under federal and state anti-fraud laws, including SEC Rule 10b-5, Advisers Act Section 206, and related SEC rules. Some of these anti-fraud laws have private rights of action by which investors can sue issuers for failure to disclose important information or for false or misleading statements and omission of material information. Fund managers and issuers should discuss with their counsel which disclosure requirements apply.

Most private funds use a private placement memorandum (PPM) that describes the management company, its key personnel, the investment thesis and plans of the fund, the features of the fund and the securities that it will issue, fees and expenses, and tax considerations, and discloses the conflicts of interest, features, and risks of the investment. Additional disclosure requirements apply to Private Funds under the Advisers Act and state securities laws. A copy of the Limited Partnership Agreement (LPA) or limited liability company operating agreement or other governing documents of the issuer normally is provided to prospective investors. Private funds operated by registered investment advisers are required to provide annual audited financial statements to investors.

Presentation and discussion of past performance information is a particularly sensitive topic and a frequent basis for SEC enforcement actions.

Discuss with your counsel the restrictions, requirements, documentation, and formatting applicable to presentation of performance information.

Broker-Dealer Registration and Regulation

Federal and state broker-dealer registration requirements apply to persons and companies engaged in the business of effecting transactions in securities. A fund manager should discuss with the fund's counsel the requirements of these laws, such as what limits to place on the compensation of fund personnel, or activities to avoid registration as securities broker-dealers in connection with the operation of a venture fund business.

A "broker" is a firm or person that acts as an agent to effect securities transactions for others. This can include an investment manager or its funds in some cases. The SEC has a non-exclusive safe harbor that allows investment management firm personnel to be engaged in the offer and sale of fund interests in private offerings, subject to several conditions.[110] Among other conditions to the exemption, the individuals must not receive commissions or bonuses based on those sales or other securities transaction-based compensation, they must have other primary functions for the manager or fund and not be predominantly involved in sales activities, they must not have worked for a securities broker-dealer within the previous 12 months, and they must not have previously been found to have violated certain laws. State securities laws may impose additional requirements, including issuer-agent licensing requirements depending on the states where the fund, the manager, and the investors are located.

A fund can hire and compensate a third-party registered broker-dealer to offer and sell interests or, in some cases, a bank or trust company that operates within an exemption from broker-dealer registration. Compensating some other type of person or firm for introducing investors to a private fund runs a variety of rescission, enforcement and litigation risks, and may put at risk the private placement and 1940 Act exemptions upon which the fund relies.

A "dealer" is a firm or person that is engaged as principal in the business of buying and selling securities for its own account. A dealer generally transacts with its customers, holding inventory, publishing quotes of prices and buying and selling at times selected by the customers to meet the needs of those customers, and in some cases providing financing and custody to those customers. An investment fund that buys and sells securities for its own account to meet its own needs and not those of others and does not make markets, publish quotes, or provide financing and custody services to customers is normally considered a "trader" rather than a "dealer" and typically is not subject to registration or regulation as a "dealer." However, in some cases the compensation or deal-making arrangements of a fund or its manager and staff can stray over the line and implicate broker-dealer registration requirements.[111]

NOTES

Chapter 10
Longevity & Growth

Chapter 10
Longevity & Growth

Looking Ahead to What Comes Next

We hope we have provided you with a bit more clarity on the components you will need to know in order to create and launch a fund you are proud of. As you begin to understand the lay of the land and become more established, shift your thinking beyond raising a fund and toward what your fund will be. As a fund manager, it is critical to know what type of firm you would like to build long-term.

There are a variety of ways to plan for your future, including succession planning, hiring, and the transfer of decision-making as you expand. Whether your goal is to spend a finite time in venture or to build a long-lasting business, we encourage you to keep these considerations in mind as you move forward.

Generally, your goal as a fund manager is to create a long-lasting business to ensure that your principles and fund live beyond you, thereby building a "Durable Franchise." Usually, this happens when you add new partners alongside the founding partners. Similar to the startup world, you will likely need to vet and convince others to join your team to carry the torch, as Durable Franchises persist well after the founding team has moved on.

Be sure to ask yourself tough questions to determine how you will follow the path of a Durable Franchise, including:

- Would you want your career in venture to be your last job?
- How long do you want to work in venture?
- When you look back in 10 years, 20 years, or more, what would you like to have accomplished professionally?
- Is there an area of the venture industry where you would like to see change?
- Do you want to have an impact on an entire investing sector?
- Is there a skillset you would like to learn after being in venture?

Without a doubt, there are other options besides developing a Durable Franchise. Another common track that fund managers pursue is Tenure Building, where you are most interested in extensive learning. Many on the "Tenure Building" path are looking to gain practical hands-on experiences that can be considered equivalent to a graduate certification, such as a Master of Business Administration (MBA) or a Chartered Financial Analyst (CFA). A third common path is "Sector Impact," where your work is highly focused on the good of the industry. If you focus on Sector Impact, for example, you may believe that Web3, deep tech, or autonomous transport will have a tremendous positive impact on the technology sector and the world.

It is very possible to move between paths or stay the course with one. Regardless of the course you take, the decision you make will have an influence on your fund's future.

Growth

Size

Be sure to consider how you will position your fund and what it means for your prospects of growth in the future. For example, if you attempt to raise a $500 million early-stage fund, investing in pre-seed and seed companies, investors may question your ability to produce meaningful returns, due to the excessive size. Similarly, if you position your fund as a generalist fund, potential investors may ask how your fund is different from other, more established funds that have come before you. Be sure to think through how the size of your fund will scale up if needed and consider adding an opportunity fund or special purpose vehicles (SPVs) to participate in more rounds.

Hiring

It is important to think about how you will scale your team. Many firms are hiring talent partners, sourcing their portfolio companies' first five hires, or finding developer talent solutions to help pull in great individuals. Decide if you will add investment professionals, operations professionals, and full-time or part-time teammates. First hires on the investment side are often scouts, venture partners, analysts, or associates. Alternatively, first hires could also be on the operations side, such as a program manager, a chief of staff, or an office manager. In the same way you would encourage your portfolio companies to find the right people, you will want to find the right individuals for your own firm. Here are some starter frameworks:

Expanding Your Operations Team

Consider whether you will hire a support team full-time within your firm and how you will find them. Investors commonly want to see additional hiring once your fund has begun to scale beyond its vintage year or the year in which your fund started making investments. As you begin to hire employees, you can make finding roles at your firm simple for candidates by using a job board such as AngelList, GoingVC, and LinkedIn. Alternatively, you may wish to work with talent partners such as Guild Talent, SCGC Search, Riviera Partners, and The Sourcery.

Expanding Your Investment Team

Consider whether you will hire another general partner to join the partnership of your investing work. Sourcing general partners can happen through your own network of strong connections, former colleagues, friends, or previous employees. Ensure that any general partner you add capably balances you and your existing skillset. In addition, you may wish to add other investment team members, either full-time or part-time, who can help expand your reach or become a part of your future succession planning. Always be mindful about deputizing affiliates to use your fund's name and clarify whether your affiliate is exclusive to your fund or not. Be sure to check with your legal counsel and confirm whether you need to inform your Limited Partner Advisory Committee (LPAC) of an affiliate or whether the addition of an affiliate could potentially fall under broker dealer violations.

Full-Time Roles

General Partner

A fund may have more than one General Partner (GP) making investment decisions. GPs are the individual owners and operators of your GP entity.

Associate

Associates are typically tasked with sourcing deals, managing deal flow, meeting Founders, and evaluating businesses.

Analyst

Analysts can take on several support roles, including deal sourcing and due diligence.

Part-Time Roles

Venture Partner

Venture partners are usually not full members of your fund's partnership. Generally, they perform deal sourcing, manage investments, and provide Board seat coverage. Venture partners often receive payment through a combination of fund carry, deal-by-deal carried interest, cash compensation, and subsidies for office space or covering student fees.

Venture Scout

Venture scouts typically help bring promising deals to your fund and have some authority to write checks. Scouts are generally not considered employees and may have other full-time jobs.

Entrepreneurs-in-Residence (EIRs)

EIRs can also help search for dealflow and are often successful entrepreneurs in between roles looking for a new company to join, incubating a new idea, or getting their feet wet in the world of venture.

As you grow your fund, be sure to think ahead and frequently review your planned future, beyond your vintage year when you start making investments. Set a plan that fits you, your fund, and your professional goals that will create a long-lasting fund.

Scan this QR code

or visit

https://www.venturefundblueprint.com/blueprints/growth

to see the interactive workbook and learn more about
The Venture Fund Blueprint

NOTES

Conclusion

Conclusion

The road to launching a fund is filled with tasks and obstacles along the way. Now that you have finished this book, you have an arsenal of tools to tackle them one step at a time. So you are probably curious: "Where do I start?"

We suggest diving right in. The journey of becoming a great fund manager only begins if you take the leap. Pull from our checklists, tips, and tricks to ensure you stay organized and hit the right milestones from the beginning.

Set your path in motion by getting ready to launch your fund, which you were introduced to in the Investment Thesis and Fund Preparation chapters (Chapters 1 and 2). Next, initiate the process of acquiring capital for your fund, which you saw broken down in the Fundraising and Limited Partner Program chapters (Chapters 3 and 4). Follow up with continual operationalizing of your fund during and after launch, which you learned about in the Portfolio Management, Operations, Fund Administration & Accounting, Portfolio Composition, and Legal chapters (Chapters 5 through 9). Then contemplate the future state of your business as you grow, which you absorbed in the Longevity & Growth chapter (Chapter 10). Finally, use the additional resources in the appendices across each chapter to apply your knowledge.

Now embark on your learning journey and walk the path to becoming a triumphant, successful, returns-generating fund manager.

Scan this QR code

or visit
https://www.venturefundblueprint.com/blueprints
/fundmanagerchecklist

to see the interactive workbook and learn more about
The Venture Fund Blueprint

Appendix

C.1 Exercise: Fund Launch Checklist

Now that you have absorbed this book's contents, you are ready to create and launch a fund focused on success, returns, and lasting value. Use the following Fund Launch Checklist to work through the list of items required and points to be considered as you kick off your fund.

Investment Thesis
- Set the long-term outlook for your fund
  - What is your focus?
  - What are your fund's principles?
  - What does success look like?
- Decide how you will achieve your vision
  - Background — List three to five strengths/interests from your background that will make you a successful investor
  - Outlook — List what macro challenges you believe portfolio companies face in the market and why are you best positioned to assist them
  - Competition — List who is directly competitive with you and why you are different
  - Investor base — Make a list of ten potential investors
  - Portfolio companies — Outline three to five potential portfolio companies

- Viability — Model/calculate minimum capital needed to raise
- Finalize investment thesis — List what type of founder/company you will invest in. List what is your differentiator/competitive advantage for how you will understand them, access them, or own more of them. State how this benefits your performance

Fund Preparation

- Understand the industry
  - Talk to ten or more individuals in the industry to understand the day-to-day of a fund manager
  - Estimate fund costs for operations
  - Set up a process for deal flow
- Establish the basic structure elements of your fund as you prepare to launch your fundraising effort
  - What is your sector?
  - What is your stage?
  - What is your average check size?
  - Will you do follow-ons?
  - Will you lead rounds?
  - Who is on your team?

Fundraising

- Create materials
  - Draft a pitch deck
  - Draft a Limited Partnership Agreement (LPA) or private placement memorandum (PPM) with your legal counsel

- Secure investors
  - Categorize the right investor prospects
  - Build a lead list
  - Gather introductions
  - Track and manage fundraising process efficiently
- Make a fundraising plan
  - Assign a point person
  - Make a timeline
  - Set a process for outreach
  - Continuously manage your lead list
  - Engage a fund formation lawyer
  - Execute your fund close
- Enable data production and management
  - Establish a data room to store pertinent documentation and information
  - Set up a customer relationship management (CRM) system

Limited Partner Program
- Develop investor relationships
  - Conduct diligence
  - Perform know your client (KYC) reviews
- Manage investor relationships
  - Keep your investors involved
  - Be transparent about both wins and losses
  - Keep fund information secure with investor portal or data room

- Set reasonable expectations around portfolio company contact
- Ensure you are following securities laws
- Schedule your investor annual meeting
- Prepare your investor updates, ideally quarterly, which should include:
  - Summary of last period
  - Portfolio company updates
  - Deal flow and pipeline
  - Recent news, publications, and hires
  - New investors
  - Milestones
  - Upcoming capital calls
  - Upcoming events
  - Upcoming fundraises for new funds
  - Opportunities to help
- Prepare for your investor annual meetings, which should include:
  - A macro overview of the fund
  - Portfolio company case studies
  - Performance updates including Internal Rate of Return (IRR)
  - Future strategy
- Deliver financial reporting to investors:
  - Quarterly valuations and financials
  - Annual valuations and financials
  - Annual K-1s

Portfolio Management

- Manage your deal flow
  - Determine a deal flow management system
  - Select a cap table management tool
  - Conduct regular due diligence
  - Establish frequent portfolio meetings
- Cultivate your investments
  - Foster relationships with portfolio companies
  - Facilitate corporate development
  - Source portfolio company talent
  - Set office hours for Founders
  - Offer an expert database of providers
  - Provide a resource for executive coaching

Operations

- Budget and review vendors for Operations Basics, including the following:
  - Fund Accounting
    - Fund administration
    - Chief Financial Officer (CFO) services
  - Fund Setup
    - Legal expenses
    - Banking expenses
    - Regulatory costs
  - Logistics

- Workspace — Office space, coworking space, leased space from another fund manager, shared space with a portfolio company or law firm
- Travel expenses
  - ○ Human Resources (HR)
    - Hiring and recruiting in-house support
  - ○ Data Management
    - Data room services
    - File hosting software
    - Customer relationship management (CRM) software
    - E-signature software
    - Information security software
    - Document sharing software
  - ○ Branding
    - Communications
    - Video conferencing
    - Website
    - Online presence
    - Public relations/publications
  - ○ Content
    - Designer for pitch deck and materials
    - Copywriter/ghost writer
- Budget and review vendors for Long-Term Operations, including the following:
  - ○ Technology
    - Task management and collaboration tools
    - Cloud computing software
    - Internet service provider

- Telecom/phone/video set up
- Virtual scheduling
  - Fund Maintenance
    - Fund insurance broker
    - Corporate credit card
    - Audit firms
    - Supplies, furniture, fixtures, and equipment
    - Research analytics
- Budget and review vendors for Growth Operations, including the following:
  - Additional HR
    - New hires
    - Payroll system/compensation
    - 401(k) benefits
  - Branding
    - Public relations (PR) and publications
  - Security
    - Home and office security systems
    - Background checks

Fund Administration & Accounting
- Address pre-formation and setup
  - Budget management fees and carry fees
  - Determine economic allocations between general partners, managing partners, venture partners, employees, etc.
  - Track management expenses versus fund expenses

- Hire fund administrator and discuss their coverage of the following:
  - Financial operations
  - Inflows and outflows
  - Fund accounting
  - Financial statements
  - Investor portals
  - K-1s
  - Tax services
- Understand financial returns
  - Performance
  - Valuation
  - Financial portfolio modeling
- Set up financial needs
  - Banking
  - Lines of credit as needed to smooth capital calls
  - Special Purpose Vehicles (SPVs)

Portfolio Composition

- Construct your fund's investment thesis
  - What is your unfair competitive advantage?
  - How will you understand/access/own companies better than others?
  - Is there an opportunity to scale?
- Build your fund model
  - What stage of companies are you investing in? For example: pre-seed, seed, Series A/B, early-stage, late-stage, growth

- What sectors and geographies are you investing in? For example: B2B, consumer, hardware, deep tech, generalist, impact
- What check sizes are you writing?
- How much in reserves will you hold for follow-on investments?

• List deal sources

- How are your deals sourced? How are your deals tracked?
- How are investment decisions made? Who and how many people are involved? Who has final say? Do you have an investment committee?

• Outline ownership andro rata rights

- Do you have pro rata ownership rights, which are the right, but not the obligation, to invest in future funding rounds? What percentage?
- How will you handle SPVs?

• Illustrate performance

- How do you demonstrate your expertise?
- Do you have an alternative demonstration of investment ability, if a "conventional" track record is not available? For example: non-traditional investing background, prior angel investments, previous operator knowledge, a foundry fund, an advisory share portfolio, a fund zero
- How do you illustrate diversity of intellect?

- Quantify case studies
  - What is a detailed historical example of your investment prowess? How did you get into the deal? What was the source?
  - When did you invest? What is your ownership? Why did you participate? Will you invest again in the next round?
  - Do you have any top-quality co-investors?
- Establish structure
  - What is your fee structure? Management fee? Carry fee?
  - What are your fees on additional deals, such as SPVs?
  - What is your capital call schedule?
- Build team
  - Who is on your team? What are your backgrounds?
  - How many GPs? What is your tenure together? What is the split percentage of ownership across your team?
  - How many employees other than GPs will you have?
- Describe purpose
  - Is your team planning for longevity? Or does your firm cease to exist if your founding team leaves?
  - Do you have an overlooked protagonist with a significant stake? Does your team have a woman, person of color, LGBTQ+, or military veteran leader?
- Define investors
  - What types of investors will you have?
  - How many investors will you have?

Legal

- Start your fund formation
  - Liaise with your fund formation lawyer
  - Engage a deal lawyer
  - Research types of fund structures
  - Understand standard and negotiable fund terms
  - Familiarize yourself with registrations and regulatory matters across state and federal
  - Identify conflicts of interest and personal investments
  - Engage a tax advisor

Longevity & Growth

- Assess what type of firm you would like to build long-term
  - Determine if and how you will achieve taking the path of building a durable franchise?
  - When you look back in 10 years, 20 years, or more, what would you like to have accomplished professionally?
- Plan for future growth
  - How will you position your fund size to continue investing?
  - What hiring will be important as you scale your team?
  - Will you expand your operations team or investment team, and will those roles be full-time or part-time?

NOTES

About the Authors

Shea Tate-Di Donna, Tate Consulting Founder;
formerly True Ventures Founding Team
Shea Tate-Di Donna is a career VC, investor, entrepreneur, advisor, and Silicon Valley insider with two decades of experience in early-stage, high tech venture capital.

Shea was Senior Vice President and part of the founding team at True Ventures. True was conceived in 2005 as the original Founders-first firm and invests in early-stage, high tech startups. The firm is known for investments in companies such as WordPress, Duo Security (acquired by Cisco), Goodreads (acquired by Amazon), Fitbit (IPO 2015), and HashiCorp (IPO 2021). Here, Shea served on the investment team and conceived True's calling card Founder Services platform. She interfaced directly with the Founders of each portfolio company and created initiatives such as True University, TEC: the True Entrepreneur Corps, and Founder Camp.

Shea has been deeply involved in the investment space and worked with a leading tech bank in Silicon Valley to head Corporate Innovation for the venture ecosystem. Here, Shea built robust products for funds to streamline capital access and operational support. Shea spearheaded a new, scalable framework for improving fund manager outcomes, now widely referred to as "Venture as a Product." Shea pioneered offerings including a unique Limited Partner Program, a Venture Lending Matching Service, and a Digital Fund Content Platform. Shea's work focused on established Emerging Manager Venture Capital (EMVC) funds, as well as what she presently defines as Transitional Emerging Manager Venture Capital (T-EMVC) funds, that are able to invest competitively at the seed and early stages. Shea has done extensive work to elevate T-EMVCs, which are an agile subset of the emerging manager ecosystem with non-traditional venture backgrounds, alternative illustrations of investment abilities and long-term track records, and diverse intellects.

Shea collaborated with a prominent family office, examining the gendered investing landscape in Silicon Valley and women's access to capital. Her extensive network includes deep connections with universities such as Duke and Stanford, accelerators such as HeavyBit and TechStars, and multiple angel groups, Micro Venture Capital (MicroVC), and early-stage VCs. She is currently an advisor to 1517 Fund, Grit Ventures, and several AI startups.

Shea was previously the Founder and CEO of Zana, a global, on-demand video and resource platform delivering skills for startup success from expert entrepreneurs. Zana was acquired by Startups.com in 2015. During the development of Zana, she taught a course at Stanford's d.school called Design Your Startup.

Shea began her career in venture with JAFCO America Ventures and then Globespan Capital Partners. Previously, she was an analyst for the CEO of Barclays North America. Shea graduated magna cum laude from Dickinson College with a BA in English and Psychology Honors and holds an MBA from Duke University's Fuqua School of Business.

Kaego Ogbechie Rust, KHOR Consulting Founder; formerly Goldman Sachs

Kaego Ogbechie Rust is a career business advisor, investor, entrepreneur, and author. With a background in financial services and over 15 years of investment experience across the public and private markets, Kaego has worked with over 1,400 companies in venture capital, private equity, hedge funds, alternative investing, startups, and small business.

Kaego is the founder and CEO of KHOR Consulting, a business advisory company focused on creating growth plans for fund managers, executive teams, and entrepreneurs. Kaego has partnered with institutions such as Goldman Sachs and the Nelson Mandela Foundation — and has worked with organizations such as Google, Facebook, Airbnb, and civic leader Former US Attorney General Eric Holder. Through her work with KHOR Consulting, Kaego has helped hundreds of companies execute their expansions by streamlining their finances, operations, and messaging.

Prior to founding KHOR Consulting, Kaego served as a Senior Vice President at Goldman Sachs for nearly ten years. During her time at Goldman Sachs, Kaego designed tactics for entry into new global markets for numerous Portfolio Managers, CEOs, and CFOs; and developed growth strategies and educational seminars for fund managers such as Tiger Global, Farallon Capital, and Partner Fund.

Kaego has been deeply involved in the investment space and worked with a leading tech bank in Silicon Valley to head Corporate Innovation for the venture ecosystem. Here, Kaego built robust products for funds to streamline capital access and operational support. Kaego spearheaded a new scalable framework for improving fund manager outcomes, now widely referred to as "Venture-as-a-Product." Kaego pioneered offerings including a unique Limited Partner Program, a Venture Lending Matching Service, and a Digital Fund Content Platform. Kaego's work focused on established Emerging Manager Venture Capital (EMVC) funds, as well as what she presently defines as Transitional Emerging Manager Venture Capital (T-EMVC) funds, that are able to invest competitively at the seed and early stages. Kaego has done extensive work to elevate T-EMVCs, which are an agile subset of the emerging manager ecosystem with non-traditional venture backgrounds, alternative illustrations of investment abilities and long-term track records, and diverse intellects.

Kaego is a regular contributing speaker and writer for a variety of publications, and her notable pieces include "How to Make a Pitch Deck for Your Fund," "How to Write an Investor Update," and "The 9-Point Due Diligence Checklist for Funds." She is a Board Member of Edgewood Center for Children and Families, the largest children's charity in the western US, and chairs its Operations Committee.

Kaego has a passion for supporting women in business, currently resides in San Francisco, and received her BA in Economics from Harvard.

Contributor Biographies

Contributor Biographies

Julie Castro Abrams, How Women Invest
Julie Castro Abrams is an expert on building boards that add a strategic advantage including proactive searches for women on corporate boards. An experienced CEO and sought-after speaker in entrepreneurship and how women lead, she is widely recognized because of her unique ability to connect people and facilitate rich conversations that make change happen.

Julie partners with terrific CEOs to build high performance, multicultural teams, in particular boards that make organizations better. She has a successful consulting practice with leaders she admires to achieve their growth and breakthrough goals.

Julie's commitment to justice and community are well known in her personal and professional endeavors. She serves as a leader on the boards of organizations focused on women and children, Latinos, economic development and the arts. Julie is a philanthropist who launched How Women Give and serves as the Governance Chair for the Women's Funding Network.

Thousands of new businesses attribute their launch and growth to her support which has resulted in millions toward the economic growth in communities. She is a leader in the country's movement to build and fund start ups.

Julie has won many awards including the Jobs Genius Award, Morgan Stanley Innovation Award, Cisco Innovation in Technology, "Women Who Could Be President" League of Women Voters, Stevie Award for Best Non Profit Executive, Human Rights Award from the Commission on the Status of Women, the Women of Color Action Network, Leadership California and the Marin Women's Hall of Fame in 2011.[112]

Raanan Bar-Cohen, Resolute Ventures

Raanan Bar-Cohen has over 18 years experience as an entrepreneur and innovator in the startup and digital media space.

Raanan Bar-Cohen is a General Partner at Resolute Ventures and is based in the San Francisco Bay Area. Before joining Resolute, Raanan was at Automattic/WordPress.com for seven years, most recently running corp dev and partnerships.

Prior to Automattic, Raanan worked at Dow Jones, Time Inc., and ran his own web agency back in the 1.0 days. Remember enhanced CDs?[113]

David Brown, Techstars

David is a serial entrepreneur who has founded three startups and been involved with two others. David is one of the original Founders of Pinpoint Technologies, Inc. which is now part of ZOLL Medical Corporation and provides solutions to the emergency medical services market. He was President of the company from founding through over $50M per year in revenue and over 250 people.

David later co-founded Techstars along with David Cohen, Brad Feld, and Jared Polis. He has been an investor and advisor to Techstars since inception. In 2013, he joined Techstars in a more active role as President.

David has a B.Sc. degree in Mathematics and Computer Science from McGill University in Montreal, Canada. As a ski instructor in the past, David still enjoys hitting the slopes on a good powder day.[114]

John Burke, PROOF and Angel Investor

John is an early-stage venture capitalist, Founder of True Ventures and passionate about growing businesses from a concept to a profitable enterprise. Having just crossed an important threshold in his professional life — having now been a venture capitalist longer than he was CEO — he still remembers what it was like to meet payroll, delight a customer, and the late nights dealing with HR issues.

He was a part of True's start in 2006 in an effort to get back to what the team was passionate about — creating strong companies. He saw an ecosystem that had lost touch with the foundation of venture capital — the early stage company. There seemed to be a lack of venture in early stage venture capital. He sought to treat the entrepreneurs that worked with True Ventures as customers, and didn't expect to make any money until the entrepreneurs and their investors did.

John is always thinking about how he can better serve our two customer sets — the entrepreneur and the investor. Whether it be while he is upland bird hunting, building a new dining room table, playing with his kids or welding in his shop — creating a more valuable company is always at the top of mind.

Specialties: Early stage (and very early stage) investing, seed investing, angel investing, startup culture, sound practical advice from someone who has been in your shoes, company formation, hunting, furniture making, flying, needlepoint and welding.[115]

Calixte Davis, Calixte Davis Design
After completing his A Levels in Art, Media and English, Cal went on to Camberwell College of Arts where he undertook an Art Foundation. He specialized in Fine Art which allowed him to explore a wealth of different mediums such as Photography, Textiles, Installation, Painting, Spoken Word, Sculpture and Audio-Visual disciplines.

Upon the completion of this Cal went to Goldsmiths College where his degree again allowed him to experiment with Animation, Radio Production, Prose Writing, Photography and Documentary Making before deciding to specialize in Script Writing and Film.

In the subsequent years he has found a happy niche in the world of graphic design, specifically Logo and Branding.

Logo design has admittedly become a passion of his. Cal loves working with a client to establish what key themes they want their logo to convey, and then making sure he executes these ideas in as clean, unique and clear a manner as possible.

Cal has been able to utilize his background and exposure to the variety of creative mediums he has been involved with to create brands and designs that stand out from the crowd.[116]

Josh Felser, Freestyle Capital

Josh is co-founder and Board Partner at Freestyle. After his time at large corporates like News Corp and Quest, he was called to the high energy and immense impact potential of entrepreneurship. He ended up co-founding Spinner and Crackle (acquired by AOL for $320M and by Sony for $65M respectively). As he thought about his next move, founding Freestyle seemed like a natural next step: early-stage investing allows Josh to harness his startup energy and help companies and CEOs grow. Most recently, Josh has been investing in startups through Climactic, his new climate-tech fund co-founded with Raj Kapoor.

Josh is a graduate of Duke University and The Fuqua School of Business.

Outside the world of venture capital, Josh can be found DJing every summer at Burning Man, hiking at Stinson, and following his daily tabata and meditation routine.[117]

John Gannon, GoingVC

Prior to joining VMTurbo John worked as an early stage VC at L Capital Partners. Earlier in his career, he worked at VMware, Scient, and FOXSports.com. John received a B.S. in Computer Science Engineering from the University of Pennsylvania and an MBA from Columbia Business School.[118]

Michael Gibson, 1517 Fund

Michael was vice president for grants at the Thiel Foundation and a principal at Thiel Capital. For nearly five years working for Peter Thiel, he has contributed research to Peter's global macro hedge fund, assisted in teaching a course at Stanford Law School on sovereignty and technological change, and helped run the Thiel Fellowship. He serves on the board of the Seasteading Institute. Before his academic apostasy, he was working towards a doctorate in philosophy at the University of Oxford. He has written on innovation and technology for MIT's Technology Review, the Atlantic, and Forbes.[119]

Jennifer Gill Roberts, Grit Ventures

Jennifer Gill Roberts is a startup investor, entrepreneur and technologist. She has over 20 years of early-stage hardware venture experiences in Silicon Valley and is known for her work founding Watermark, the leading organization for women entrepreneurs. Before her career in venture, Jennifer led product and technical efforts at Apple, HP and Sun Microsystems. Jennifer is an active Stanford alum (GSB and SOE) and a mentor at Stanford's StartX incubator, the Stanford Venture Studio, and ICME at the School of Engineering. Jennifer also serves on the JCEI West Coast Advisory Board for Indiana University and is a Senior Fellow of the American Leadership Forum. She holds a BSEE from Stanford, an MSEE from UT and an MBA from Stanford.[120]

Tracy Gray, The 22 Fund

Innovative & visionary leader, systems changer, and barrier breaker with solid international, investment, business strategy and marketing experience. Exceptional due diligence, analytical and communication skills. Relationship builder across a variety of industries — from technology to venture capital to entertainment.

Tracy Gray is the Founder and Managing Partner of The 22 Fund (The 22), an impact, early growth venture capital/private equity firm with a mission of creating the clean, quality jobs of the future by increasing the global competitiveness of manufacturing companies, intentionally targeting women- and BIPOC-owned businesses. She is a Board Director for Applife Digital Solutions, Inc (ALDS), a publicly-traded, fully-reporting, start-up incubator/ venture studio, and the California State University, Dominguez Hills Philanthropic Foundation Endowment. She is also a Lead Partner at Portfolia Green & Sustainability Fund and an Executive-in-Residence at the Los Angeles Cleantech Incubator (LACI). She is the first Social Impact Fellow at the UC Berkeley Haas Business School's Center for Equity, Gender, and Leadership. After giving a TEDx Talk entitled "Why It's Time for Women to Be Sexist with Investment Capital," Ms. Gray founded the non-profit We Are Enough. WAE's mission is to educate ALL women on how and why to invest in women-owned, for-profit businesses or with a gender lens. Ms. Gray is featured in the recently released book "200 Women: Who Will Change the Way You See the World" and received the Bad Ass Woman in Green award from the California League of Conservation Voters.[121]

Kirsten Green, Forerunner Ventures

Combining a unique and unconventional blend of professional history and acquired investment experience, Kirsten launched San Francisco-based Forerunner Ventures in 2010, where she serves as Founder and Managing Director. Noticing that emerging purchasing processes were linear and ripe for improvement, Kirsten developed a pacesetter mentality and analytical eye to remain ahead of experience-driven retail trends and identify compelling brand platforms and visionary entrepreneurs.

In an unpredictable consumer landscape, Kirsten's 20+ years of evaluation and investment success stems from a combination of product savvy, retail acumen and a thesis-driven approach that has been the basis of all her investments — from pre-revenue startups to multi-billion-dollar enterprises — to date. As a Founder, Kirsten has led efforts to raise over $650M+ from leading investors and has invested in more than 80 companies. She currently serves as a member of the Board of Directors at Glossier, Outdoor Voices, Ritual, Inturn, and Indigo Fair, among other Forerunner portfolio companies. She also served on the board of Dollar Shave Club and Bonobos, two Forerunner portfolio companies with notable sale transactions.

Kirsten has been honored in Time's 100 Most Influential People, named a Top 20 Venture Capitalists by The New York Times in 2018 & 2017, is part of Forbes' 2020, 2019, 2018 & 2017 Midas Lists, in addition to being named in the magazine's World's 100 Most Powerful Women. She has been named VC of the Year at TechCrunch's 2017 Crunchies Awards and listed on Vanity Fair's New Establishment list. Kirsten is a founding member of the female mentorship collective, All Raise, and champions women in the tech industry, recently giving a SXSW Keynote speech on diversity in a male-dominated industry.

Prior to Forerunner, Kirsten was an equity research analyst and investor at Banc of America Securities, formerly Montgomery Securities, covering publicly-traded retail and consumer stocks. Kirsten graduated from UCLA with a B.A. in Business Economics, and has earned a CPA license and a CFA certification.[122]

Charles Hudson, Precursor Ventures

Charles Hudson is the Managing Partner and Founder of Precursor Ventures, an early-stage venture capital firm focused on investing in the first institutional round of investment for the most promising software and hardware companies.

Prior to founding Precursor Ventures, Charles was a Partner at SoftTech VC. In this role, he focused on identifying investment opportunities in mobile infrastructure.[123]

Jim Jensen, Wilson Sonsini Goodrich & Rosati

James (Jim) Jensen is a partner in the Palo Alto office of Wilson Sonsini Goodrich & Rosati, where his practice focuses on forming and representing investment funds, acting as outside general counsel to start-up companies, and advising on related regulatory matters. During Jim's 20 years of practice, he has been involved in more than 500 investment fund and start-up company transactions and is known for his solutions-oriented and practical perspective.

For his fund services practice, Jim advises venture capital funds, angel investment funds, accelerators/incubators, SPVs (series LLCs and stand-alone), funds-of-funds and other private equity funds in connection with structuring, formation, and operations, including their venture capital investments in startup companies. In addition to deep experience advising established investment fund sponsors, Jim has significant experience working with first-time fund managers who are raising smaller funds. He also represents institutional investors in connection with their investments in investment funds, including reviewing limited partnership agreements and negotiating side letters.

For his start-up company practice, he represents start-up and emerging growth companies at all stages of development. He has represented multiple companies from formation to exit, whether IPO or M&A. His clients include companies across a diverse range of industries, including digital media, Internet, esports, biotech, mobile, security, and software. He occasionally represents non-technology companies in various sectors, including companies focusing on coffee, tea, and restaurant services.

For his regulatory practice, Jim advises investment funds and start-up companies regarding their relevant regulatory obligations, including relevant exclusions or exemptions, under the Securities Act, Securities Exchange Act, Investment Advisers Act, and Investment Company Act.

Jim is also a technology entrepreneur and has formed and managed several e-commerce and other Internet companies through exit and is currently working on a legal tech start-up in beta mode. He regularly speaks at various professional and industry events, as well as at nationally recognized universities, and serves as a judge at start-up pitch events.

Prior to rejoining the firm in 2018, Jim was a partner at Perkins Coie, where he led the fund services practice in the Bay Area, and a member of the emerging companies and venture capital practice. Previously, from 2005 to 2011, he served as general counsel of emerging markets at VantagePoint Capital Partners, an investment fund with approximately $5 billion under management, where he managed hundreds of investment transactions. From 1999 to 2005, he was a fund services and corporate associate at Wilson Sonsini. Before entering the legal industry, Jim served as the chief financial officer at Penta Press, where he managed accounting, finance, human resource, and purchasing professionals, among other duties.[124]

Eric Krichevsky, RYLNYC

Eric Krichevsky is the founder of RYLNYC.[125]

Scott Kupor, Andreessen Horowitz

Scott Kupor is the managing partner at Andreessen Horowitz, where he is responsible for all operational aspects of running the firm. He has been with the firm since its inception in 2009 and has overseen its rapid growth, from three employees to more than 150+ and from $300 million in assets under management to more than $10 billion.

Prior to joining Andreessen Horowitz, Scott worked as vice president and general manager of software as a service at Hewlett-Packard. Scott joined HP in 2007 as part of the Opsware acquisition, where he was senior vice president of customer solutions. In this role, he had global responsibility for customer interaction, including professional services, technical pre-sales, and customer support. Scott joined Opsware shortly after the company's founding and held numerous executive management positions, including vice president of financial planning and vice president of corporate development. In these roles, he led the company's private financing activities as well as its initial public offering in 2001. Scott also started the company's Asia Pacific operations and led the execution of the company's multiple acquisitions.

Prior to Opsware, Scott represented software companies in both financing and mergers and acquisitions transactions at Credit Suisse First Boston and Lehman Brothers. He graduated Phi Beta Kappa from Stanford University with a bachelor's degree in public policy with honors and distinction. Scott also holds a law degree with distinction from Stanford University and is a member of the State Bar of California. Scott is chairman of the Board of Genesys Works; co-Founder and co-director of the Stanford Venture Capital Director's College; co-Founder and co-director of the Stanford Rock Center's Guide to Venture-Backed Board Membership; executive-in-residence at Haas School of Business and Boalt School of Law; and a lecturer at Stanford Law School. He is vice-chair of the investment committee of St. Jude's Children's Cancer Research Hospital and also serves as a member of the investment committees for Stanford Medical Center, the Silicon Valley Community Foundation, and Lick Wilmerding High School.

Scott served as chairman of the Board of the National Venture Capital Association (2017–2018). He is the author of the nationally bestselling book *Secrets of Sand Hill Road: Venture Capital and How to Get It*, published by Portfolio, a division of Penguin.[126]

Frances Luu, formerly Storm Ventures

Frances Luu is a career VC operation and community leader with an expertise in early stage venture capital. With her exposure to early stage startup companies, along with portfolio management experience for over 180 enterprise companies, Frances has managed the deal pipeline of companies from their series A funding to exit.

Frances served as an Executive Assistant to the Founding Managing Directors of Storm Ventures. While leading the operational and administrative efforts for the team, she drove the revival of the firm's culture and brand. The creation of an approachable and collaborative environment within the firm enabled Founders to build and receive access to the right tools to expand their company.

During her time at Storm Ventures, Frances strategized and implemented a Founder community for the firm's ecosystem of entrepreneurs through curated touchpoints featuring industry leaders such as Kim Scott (Radical Candor), Sean Kanuck (US Intelligence Analyst), and Jacco vander Kooij (Winning by Design). The success of the touchpoints increased the firm's presence and presented the firm as thought leaders in the enterprise space.

Frances also played a key role in the inception of the book series called "Survival to Thrival, Building Enterprise Startups." As the production manager of the series with Mascot Books Publishing Company, she curated and designed graphics for the series, as well as produced the series' marketing assets. The success of the book series led to the inception of the Go-To-Market Fit Summit in San Francisco, several accolades from startups and accelerators across the world, and high ranks on Amazon books and Goodreads.

Prior to Storm Ventures, Frances graduated from San Francisco State University with a BA in Biology.[127]

Julie Mauser, LifeSci Venture Partners

Julie joins LifeSci with more than 10 years of experience working with institutional investors. Most recently, Julie was Head of Business Development at Atrato Advisors, an outsourced consultant for alternative investments. Prior to Atrato Advisors, Julie was Vice President of Marketing at Par-Four Investment Management, a credit-focused alternative investment manager. At Par-Four, she coordinated marketing and investor relations, cultivating relationships with family office and institutional clients. Previously, Julie was part of the Capital Introduction team at Jefferies & Company, where she was in charge of growing and maintaining the firm's relationships with family office investors. She started her career as a member of JP Morgan's prime brokerage team.

Julie grew up competitive figure skating and continues her love of the sport by volunteering to coach NYC elementary school children who are learning to skate. She graduated magna cum laude from Lehigh University with a Bachelor of Science degree in Marketing.[128]

Matt McInerney, Township

Matt approaches every project with the goal of delivering elegant and deliberate design. He's at his best in the middle of a puzzle that he needs to design his way out of. An alum of Pentagram, Matt is now part of the Township leadership and has his hands in every project. You can also hear him ramble on a podcast every now and then.[129]

Alison Rosenthal, Leadout Capital

Alison is the Founder and managing partner of Leadout Capital, an early stage venture capital firm. Ali was one of Facebook's earliest business hires where she helped to found the cross-functional Facebook Mobile team, responsible for building and scaling the mobile user base to hundreds of millions during her time at the company. Most recently, she was the VP of Partnerships and Brokerage Ops at Wealthfront. She currently serves as an independent director on the board of AutoNation (NYSE: AN) where she also chairs the Technology Committee.

Ali's early career is comprised of financial analytics and investment roles at Goldman Sachs (M&A), General Atlantic Partners, and Greylock Partners.

Ali is also an angel investor, served in the Obama Administration as a PAGE Fellow, was a pro cyclist and lives in Northern California with her wife and two kiddos.[130]

Jason Rowley, Capbase

Jason D. Rowley is an entrepreneur and researcher based in Chicago. He published the first words on Crunchbase News.[131]

Roberto Sanabria, Expa

Roberto Sanabria is Managing Partner of Expa, overseeing the company's day-to-day operations and working closely on early stage projects. Previously, Roberto held business analytics and finance roles at LinkedIn, StumbleUpon, and Google. Roberto was born in Venezuela.[132]

Michael Seibel, Y Combinator

Michael Seibel was the co-Founder and CEO of Justin.tv and Socialcam. Socialcam sold to Autodesk in 2012 and under the leadership of Emmett Shear, Justin.tv became Twitch.tv and sold to Amazon in 2014. Before getting into startups, he spent a year as the finance director for a US Senate campaign and in 2005, Michael graduated from Yale University with a BA in political science.[133]

Danielle Strachman, 1517 Fund

Danielle is a co-Founder and general partner of 1517. She has worked with young entrepreneurs for about a decade. In 2010, during the founding of the Thiel Fellowship, Danielle joined to lead the design and operations. She's worked with some of the most prestigious Founders like Vitalik Buterin and Ritesh Agarwal. Previous to her work with Peter Thiel,

Danielle founded and directed Innovations Academy in San Diego, a K-8 charter school serving 400 students, with a focus on student-led project based learning and other alternative programs.[134]

Adam Tope, DPA Piper

Adam Tope provides leading secondaries firms, investment fund sponsors, and investors with creative, commercial and realistic advice relating to fund formation and GP-led transactions. He brings a global perspective to his clients, having represented managers and investors in dozens of jurisdictions.

Adam's secondaries practice is primarily focused on representing lead investors in connection with GP-led transactions such as continuation funds, tender offers and other complex secondary transactions. He also specializes in representing spin out teams in GP-led spin out transactions, particularly in the energy and venture capital space. Adam has completed over 100 secondaries transactions in his career and has developed class-leading efficient processes to manage tender offers and pooled sale/purchase transactions for leading secondaries investors, endowments and sovereign wealth funds.

Adam's sponsor-side clients regularly include prominent private equity and hedge fund managers, real estate managers, and venture capital sponsors. He advises these clients with entity formation, introductions to service providers, discussions with placement agents, drafting of offering memorandums, negotiations with investors and Investment Advisers Act and Investment Company Act compliance, as well as guidance on ongoing operational funds. Adam also draws on his experience as a former computer programmer to advise fund managers forming cryptofunds. Adam has a particular niche representing first time managers and spin outs — handling every aspect of the spin out including employment and track record issues with the prior firm, setting up management companies and assisting in fundraising and formation of first-time funds. Adam has worked with spin outs from Apollo, Carlyle, Riverstone, Summit Partners and others. Adam also regularly represents fund principals with respect to the negotiation of their employment arrangements with funds. He has a deep understanding of how principal compensation is structured and can guide principals with the negotiation of vesting arrangements, key person/for cause removal rights, and rights to carried interest/promote.

Adam lastly has a prominent practice of investor-side clients including family offices, funds of funds, endowments, sovereign wealth funds and royal families. He has represented these investors in hundreds of transactions in nearly every jurisdiction and in nearly every type of fund. These transactions include investments into private equity funds, hedge funds, venture capital funds, funds of funds, SBIC funds and hybrid funds. This work also includes representing investors in complicated secondary transactions, managed accounts, co-investments, funds of ones, joint ventures and other bespoke alternatives transactions.

Outside of the investment funds universe, Adam is a former serial entrepreneur, having served as the president and CEO of a technology incubator that was ranked as one of the 500 largest online companies — giving him an entrepreneurial perspective useful to first-time funds, startups and venture-backed organizations.[135]

Eric Woo, Revere

Eric is co-founder and CEO of Revere, where he leads product development and investment analysis & due diligence efforts.

Prior to starting Revere, he was Head of Institutional Capital at AngelList, the world's largest online venture capital investment platform that supports over $10B in assets and has participated in the financing of over 190 "unicorn" companies. At AngelList, Eric worked closely with investors to curate early-stage fund and deal opportunities. He also developed systematic and data-driven strategies for institutional investors.

Over the last 12 years, Eric has helped allocate over $160 million in venture funds and direct co-investments. Notably, he played a key role in establishing the emerging manager investment programs at Top Tier Capital and Northgate Capital, organizations that collectively have more than $15B in AUM. Eric is an acknowledged thought leader in the VC emerging managers ecosystem.

Before his venture career, Eric worked in pricing and risk management for a large insurance company and financial guarantor. He also has experience in online marketing and private markets research. A Bay Area native, Eric graduated with a B.S. degree in Mechanical Engineering from UC Berkeley and has been a CFA charter holder since 2004.[136]

Lan Xuezhao, Basis Set Ventures

Founding and Managing Partner. Lan built and led the Corporate Development Strategy team at Dropbox during its most acquisitive time. She previously managed teams at McKinsey in New York and Shanghai, advising

Fortune 500 companies on issues including big data, AI, and growth strategy. Earlier in her career, Lan designed and developed brain training games as a founder and studied human brain functions for her Ph.D. She also received her M.A. in Statistics, both from the University of Michigan.[137]

Alan Yang, Towne Advisory Services
Principal and Director of Accounting Services at Towne Advisory Services Corp.[138]

Elizabeth Yin, Hustle Fund
General Partner and Co-Founder at Hustle Fund. Ex-Partner at 500 Startups. Ex-Googler. Founder of LaunchBit (acquired 2014). Founder of Hustle Con. Stanford BA 2004. MIT MBA 2007.[139]

Timothy Young, Dropbox
Tim is an entrepreneur, executive, and investor focused on early-stage technology.

Tim builds and invests in companies that are authentic to who he is. He is obsessed with transforming the way people work (Socialcast / VMware / Dropbox). Tim was named one of Forbes "10 Rising Stars at the World's Most Innovative Companies" (No. 3 while @ VMware).

He has a unique background in that he has founded and successfully exited both enterprise and consumer software startups. He founded the enterprise collaboration platform, Socialcast (acquired by VMware for over $100M) and co-founded About.me (acquired by AOL) where he gained valuable operational experience. He has operated large scale business units with >1000 employees and ~$1.5B in revenue. After an executive role at VMware, he currently builds and invests in very early-stage technology projects particularly those focused on enterprise apps and crypto-assets.

His specialties include: Start-Up Businesses; Venture Capital; Enterprise Collaboration; Very Early Stage Venture Capital; Seed Stage Investing; Startup Advice; Enterprise Software; Blockchain; Cryptocurrency; Technology Investing; Coaching; Consumer Internet; Business Development; New Product Development; Mergers and Acquisitions.[140]

Endnotes

Chapter 1

1 Preqin, n.d., https://www.preqin.com.

2 Michael Gibson, personal interview; Danielle Strachman, personal interview.

3 Jennifer Gill-Roberts, personal interview.

4 Raanan Bar-Cohen, personal interview.

5 Sequoia Capital US/Europe, n.d., https://www.sequoiacap.com/our-ethos.

6 "Y Combinator," Crunchbase, n.d., https://www.crunchbase.com/organization /y-combinator#section-overview; "Y Combinator," Y Combinator, n.d., https://www .ycombinator.com; Michael Seibel, personal interview; Alex Wilhelm, "Listen to Equity's Interview with YC CEO Michael Seibel," Crunchbase News, August 20, 2019, https://news .crunchbase.com/venture/listen-to-equitys-interview-with-yc-ceo-michael-seibel.

Chapter 2

7 Crunchbase, n.d., https://www.crunchbase.com; Jason Rowley, Rep, *Emerging Venture Data, Crunchbase Report*, n.d.; PitchBook, n.d., https://pitchbook.com; Statista, n.d., https://www.statista.com.

8 Preqin, n.d., https://www.preqin.com/.

9 Scott Kupor, personal interview.

10 Charles Hudson, personal interview.

Chapter 3

11 Preqin, n.d., https://www.preqin.com/.

12 Elizabeth Yin, "How I Raised My $11.5m VC Fund," Elizabeth Yin, December 21, 2018, https://elizabethyin.com/2018/12/19/how-i-raised-my-11-5m-vc-fund.

13 SEC.gov, n.d., https://www.sec.gov.

14 Elizabeth Yin, personal interview.

15 Lan Xuezhao, personal interview.

16 Alison Rosenthal, personal interview.

17 Kirsten Green, personal interview.

18 Roger Ehrenberg, "Building a Seed Stage Venture Firm," Medium, February 24, 2019, https://infoarbitrage.medium.com/building-a-seed-stage-venture-firm-c432816ce45e.

19 Pejman Nozad, "Tech's Most Unlikely Venture Capitalist," Medium, February 2, 2016, https://pejmannozad.medium.com/tech-s-most-unlikely-venture-capitalist-bb002488f297.

20 Elizabeth Yin, "How I Raised My $11.5m VC Fund," Elizabeth Yin, December 21, 2018, https://elizabethyin.com/2018/12/19/how-i-raised-my-11-5m-vc-fund/.

21 "How to Fund a Startup," Paul Graham, n.d., http://paulgraham.com/startupfunding.html.

22 Fred Wilson, "What Is a 'Venture Partner' and Why Does It Matter to You?" AVC, August 7, 2010, https://avc.com/2010/08/what-is-a-venture-partner-and-does-it-matter-to-you.

23 Mark Suster, "Some Advice before You Hit the Fund Raising Trail," Medium, Both Sides of the Table, May 6, 2018, https://bothsidesofthetable.com/some-advice-before-you-hit-the-fund-raising-trail-73dc646f077e.

Chapter 4

24 "2021 Partner's Instructions for Schedule K-1 (Form 1065)," n.d., https://www.irs.gov/pub/irs-pdf/i1065sk1.pdf.

25 Frances Luu, personal interview.

Chapter 5

26 There are many definitions of Emerging Manager Venture Capital (EMVC) that vary or have additional parameters. EMVC funds are generally a subset of Venture Capital firms that seek equity or equity-linked investments in privately held, high-growth startups and small to medium-sized enterprises with strong growth potential. When defining EMVC, some industry participants use the amount of assets under management (AUM), the number of funds, or even years of investing experience to describe the category. Industry norms commonly characterize an EMVC fund as sub $1bb-$2bb AUM, approximately $100-$250mm per fund, fewer than four funds, and a five- to ten-year track record. A common misconception is that EMVC encompasses only first-time fund managers, but we see a broad swath of fund managers, ranging across experience, variety, and investment focus. It should also be noted that EMVC can potentially include accelerators, incubators, or studios that fit the above-mentioned qualifiers. Although nomenclature commonly used in the industry includes Micro Venture Capital (MicroVC; less than $100mm) and Nano Venture Capital

(NanoVC; less than $25mm), some definitions of MicroVC and NanoVC may vary or have additional parameters — for example, some industry participants use a number of funds or even years of investing experience to define MicroVC and NanoVC.

27 Mark Boslet and -, "The New Full-Service VC," Venture Capital Journal, June 1, 2013, https://www.venturecapitaljournal.com/the-new-full-service-vc.

28 Mark Boslet and -, "The New Full-Service VC," Venture Capital Journal, June 1, 2013, https://www.venturecapitaljournal.com/the-new-full-service-vc.

29 Andreessen Horowitz, n.d., https://a16z.com; First Round Capital, n.d., https://firstround .com; Mark Boslet and -, "The New Full-Service VC," Venture Capital Journal, June 1, 2013, https://www.venturecapitaljournal.com/the-new-full-service-vc.; SEC.gov, n.d., https://www.sec.gov; True Ventures, n.d., https://trueventures.com.

30 "Articles: First Round Review," Articles | First Round Review, n.d., https://review.firstround .com/articles; "First Round Essentials: Management," First Round, n.d., https://books .firstround.com/management; "First Round State of Startups 2019," First Round State of Startups 2019, n.d., https://stateofstartups2019.firstround.com; Capital, First Round, First Round Holiday Video 2017, n.d., http://holiday.firstround.com; Daniel Terdiman, "After 'Me Too," Men and Women Disagree on Solutions to Sexual Harassment at Startups," Fast Company, Fast Company, December 6, 2017, https://www.fastcompany.com/4050 4570/after-me-too-men-and-women-disagree-on-solutions-to-sexual-harassment-at -startups?utm_content=bufferb2748; Erin Griffith, "Many Startup Founders Doubt Extent of Sexual Harassment," Wired, Conde Nast, December 6, 2017, https://www.wired.com /story/many-startup-founders-doubt-extent-of-sexual-harassment; Zoë Bernard, "What It Was like to Work at Startups in 2017, According to over 850 Founders Surveyed by a Top VC Firm," Business Insider, Business Insider, December 6, 2017, https://www.businessinsider.com/state-of-startups-2017-according-to-over-850 -founders-first-round-capital-2017-12.

31 PitchBook, n.d., https://pitchbook.com.

32 First Round Capital, n.d., https://firstround.com.

33 "First Round State of Startups 2019," First Round State of Startups 2019, n.d., https://stateofstartups2019.firstround.com

34 "Articles: First Round Review," Articles | First Round Review, n.d., https://review .firstround.com/articles; "First Round Essentials: Management," First Round, n.d., https://books.firstround.com/management.

35 Daniel Terdiman, "After 'Me Too," Men and Women Disagree on Solutions to Sexual Harassment at Startups," Fast Company, Fast Company, December 6, 2017, https://www.fastcompany.com/40504570/after-me-too-men-and-women-disagree -on-solutions-to-sexual-harassment-at-startups?utm_content=bufferb2748; Erin Griffith, "Many Startup Founders Doubt Extent of Sexual Harassment," Wired, Conde Nast,

December 6, 2017, https://www.wired.com/story/many-startup-founders-doubt-extent
-of-sexual-harassment; Zoë Bernard, "What It Was like to Work at Startups in 2017,
According to over 850 Founders Surveyed by a Top VC Firm," Business Insider, Business
Insider, December 6, 2017, https://www.businessinsider.com/state-of-startups-2017
-according-to-over-850-founders-first-round-capital-2017-12.

36 Capital, First Round, First Round Holiday Video 2017, n.d., http://holiday.firstround.com.

37 Crunchbase, n.d., https://www.crunchbase.com/.

38 True Ventures, n.d., https://trueventures.com/.

39 "Founder Camp 2014," True Ventures, n.d., https://trueventures.com/blog/founder
-camp-2014.

40 "True University," True Ventures, n.d., https://trueventures.com/true-platform/university.

41 "True Ventures Fellowship," True Ventures, n.d., https://trueventures.com/true-platform
/fellowships/tec.

42 "Briefings," Andreessen Horowitz, n.d., https://a16z.com/briefings; "Our Summit Events
Archives," Andreessen Horowitz, n.d., https://a16z.com/tag/a16z-summits; Deborah Gage,
"Why Andreessen Horowitz Models Itself After A Hollywood Talent Agency," The Wall
Street Journal, Dow Jones & Company, January 21, 2011, https://www.wsj.com/articles
/BL-VCDB-10148.

43 Andreessen Horowitz, n.d., https://a16z.com; Silicon Investor (SI) -- Stock Discussion
Forums, n.d., http://www.siliconinvestor.com.

44 Andreessen Horowitz, n.d., https://a16z.com.

45 Andreessen Horowitz, n.d., https://a16z.com.

46 Maya Rahkonen, personal interview.

47 "Our Summit Events Archives," Andreessen Horowitz, n.d., https://a16z.com/tag/a16z-
summits/.

48 "Briefings," Andreessen Horowitz, n.d., https://a16z.com/briefings/.

49 Amy Simmerman and Steve Bochner, "The Venture Capital Board Member's Survival Guide,"
The Harvard Law School Forum on Corporate Governance, December 15, 2016,
https://corpgov.law.harvard.edu/2016/12/15/the-venture-capital-board-members
-survival-guide; SEC.gov, n.d., https://www.sec.gov.

50 Mark Suster, "Startup Boards," Medium, Both Sides of the Table, April 7, 2019,
https://bothsidesofthetable.com/startup-boards-ee3ad0389040.

51 Expa, n.d., https://www.expa.com.

52 Josh Felser, personal interview.

53 "Venture Capital Due Diligence: The Scorecard," GoingVC, n.d., https://www.goingvc
.com/post/venture-capital-due-diligence-the-scorecard.

54 "Venture Capital Due Diligence: Financial Valuation," GoingVC, n.d., https://www.goingvc
.com/post/venture-capital-due-diligence-financial-valuation.

55 "Venture Capital Due Diligence: The Scorecard." GoingVC, n.d., https://www.goingvc
.com/post/venture-capital-due-diligence-the-scorecard.

Chapter 6

56 "Health Insurance Marketplace." HealthCare.gov, n.d. https://www.healthcare.gov;
"Internal Revenue Service." Internal Revenue Service, n.d., https://www.irs.gov/.

57 Frances Luu, personal interview.

Chapter 7

58 Asher Bearman, "How VC Funds Work — Structure Chart for Venture Capital Fund
(US Fund)," The Venture Alley, February 27, 2011, https://www.theventurealley.com
/2011/02/how-vc-funds-work-typical-fund-structure/.

59 Aduro Advisors, n.d., https://www.aduroadvisors.com/; Carta, n.d., https://www.carta
.com/; Cornerstone Fund Services, n.d., https://cornerstonefundservices.com/; Standish
Management, n.d., https://www.standishmanagement.com/.

60 Angel Investor, personal interview.

61 Anonymous, personal interview.

62 Michael Gibson, personal interview; Danielle Strachman, personal interview.

63 Kirsten Green, personal interview.

64 Nick Moran. "A Simple Capitalization Table Template." Eloquens, n.d. https://www
.eloquens.com/tool/PlDuwG/startups/cap-tables/a-simple-capitalization-table-template.

65 "Capitalization Table Excel Template," Eloquens, n.d., https://www.eloquens.com/tool
/zRNsbJ/startups/cap-tables/capitalization-table-excel-template.

66 "Venture Capital Jobs and Career Resources (2022 Edition)," Venture Capital Newsletter
and VC Jobs, July 31, 2022, https://johngannonblog.com/.

67 "Venture Capital Fund ProForma Financial Statements Reference Manual," Withum, n.d.,
https://www.withum.com/wp-content/uploads/2016/01/Venture-Capital-Fund-Dec
20151.pdf.

68 "Venture Capital Fund ProForma Financial Statements Reference Manual," Withum, n.d.,
https://www.withum.com/wp-content/uploads/2016/01/Venture-Capital-Fund-Dec
20151.pdf.

69 "Venture Capital Fund ProForma — Financial Statements Reference Manual," Withum, n.d., https://www.withum.com/wp-content/uploads/2016/01/Venture-Capital-Fund-Dec20151.pdf.

70 "Venture Capital Ecosystem," GoingVC, n.d., https://www.goingvc.com/.

71 Asher Bearman, "How VC Funds Work — Structure Chart for Venture Capital Fund (US Fund)," The Venture Alley, February 27, 2011, https://www.theventurealley.com/2011/02/how-vc-funds-work-typical-fund-structure/.

72 Ahmad Takatkah, "VC Funds 101: Understanding Venture Fund Structures, Team Compensation, Fund Metrics and Reporting," Medium, VCpreneur, April 16, 2019, https://vcpreneur.com/vc-funds-101-understanding-venture-fund-structures-team-compensation-fund-metrics-and-reporting-152b02e8504a.

Chapter 8

73 Crunchbase, n.d., https://www.crunchbase.com/; Jason Rowley, Rep, *Emerging Venture Data, Crunchbase Report*, n.d.; PitchBook, n.d., https://pitchbook.com/; Statista, n.d., https://www.statista.com/.

74 Investopedia, n.d. https://www.investopedia.com/; Josh Lerner, Ann Leamon, and Felda Hardymon, "Venture Capital, Private Equity, and the Financing of Entrepreneurship," Venture Capital, Private Equity, and the Financing of Entrepreneurship — Harvard Business School, n.d., https://www.hbs.edu/faculty/Pages/item.aspx?num=37305.

75 Note that although nomenclature commonly referred to in the industry includes Micro Venture Capital (MicroVC) (sub $100mm) and Nano Venture Capital (NanoVC) (sub $25mm), some definitions of MicroVC and NanoVC may vary or have additional parameters, for example, some industry participants use the number of funds or even years of investing experience to define MicroVC and NanoVC. Across the many industry definitions of EMVC, we see a broad swath of fund managers, ranging across experience, diversity, and investment focus. It should also be noted that some industry definitions of EMVC, MicroVC, and NanoVC include accelerators, incubators, and studios that fit the aforementioned qualifiers.

76 Preqin, n.d., https://www.preqin.com/.

77 Jason Rowley, Rep, *Emerging Venture Data, Crunchbase Report*, n.d.

78 Nikhil Basu Trivedi, "The Rise of the Solo Capitalists," July 8, 2020, https://nbt.substack.com/p/the-rise-of-the-solo-capitalists?s=r.

79 Jason Rowley, Rep, *Emerging Venture Data, Crunchbase Report*, n.d.

80 Jason Rowley, Rep, *Emerging Venture Data, Crunchbase Report*, n.d.

81 Jason Rowley, Rep, *Emerging Venture Data, Crunchbase Report*, n.d.

82 Crunchbase, n.d. https://www.crunchbase.com/; Jason Rowley. Rep. *Emerging Venture Data, Crunchbase Report*, n.d.

83 Crunchbase, n.d. https://www.crunchbase.com/; Jason Rowley. Rep. *Emerging Venture Data, Crunchbase Report*, n.d.

84 Crunchbase, n.d. https://www.crunchbase.com/; Jason Rowley. Rep. *Emerging Venture Data, Crunchbase Report*, n.d.

85 Mike Freeman, "Seed Stage Funding Crunch Coming?" Innosphere Ventures, March 11, 2021, https://innosphereventures.org/seedstagecrunch/; PitchBook, n.d., https://pitchbook.com/.

86 "How to Manage a 80+ Portfolio with a <5 Person Team — Airtable Universe," Airtable, n.d., https://www.airtable.com/universe/exp3iBIEpdjB3pGVk/how-to-manage-a-80 -portfolio-with-a-less5-person-team?explore=true.

87 "How to Manage a 80+ Portfolio with a <5 Person Team — Airtable Universe," Airtable, n.d., https://www.airtable.com/universe/exp3iBIEpdjB3pGVk/how-to-manage-a-80 -portfolio-with-a-less5-person-team?explore=true.

88 Jerry Neumann, "Power Laws in Venture Portfolio Construction," Reaction Wheel, April 8, 2021, http://reactionwheel.net/2017/12/power-laws-in-venture-portfolio-construction .html; Rodrigo Ferreira, "An LP Take on VC Portfolio Construction," Find the best investors for your startup, March 28, 2022, https://openvc.app/blog/vc-portfolio-construction.

89 Jerry Neumann, "Power Laws in Venture Portfolio Construction," Reaction Wheel, April 8, 2021, http://reactionwheel.net/2017/12/power-laws-in-venture-portfolio-construction .html; Rodrigo Ferreira, "An LP Take on VC Portfolio Construction," Find the best investors for your startup, March 28, 2022, https://openvc.app/blog/vc-portfolio-construction.

90 Jerry Neumann, "Power Laws in Venture Portfolio Construction," Reaction Wheel, April 8, 2021, http://reactionwheel.net/2017/12/power-laws-in-venture-portfolio-construction .html; Rodrigo Ferreira, "An LP Take on VC Portfolio Construction," Find the best investors for your startup, March 28, 2022, https://openvc.app/blog/vc-portfolio-construction.

Chapter 9

91 Preqin, n.d., https://www.preqin.com/; PitchBook, n.d., https://pitchbook.com/; SEC.gov, n.d., https://www.sec.gov/; LexisNexis, n.d., https://www.lexisnexis.com/en-us/gateway .page; Investopedia, n.d., https://www.investopedia.com/; Oxford English Dictionary, n.d., https://www.oed.com/; Merriam-Webster, n.d., https://www.merriam-webster.com.

92 Angel Investor, personal interview.

93 Preqin, n.d., https://www.preqin.com/; PitchBook, n.d., https://pitchbook.com/; SEC.gov, n.d., https://www.sec.gov/; LexisNexis, n.d., https://www.lexisnexis.com/en-us/gateway

.page; Investopedia, n.d., https://www.investopedia.com/; Oxford English Dictionary, n.d., https://www.oed.com/; Merriam-Webster, n.d., https://www.merriam-webster.com.

94 Preqin, n.d., https://www.preqin.com/; PitchBook, n.d., https://pitchbook.com/; SEC.gov, n.d., https://www.sec.gov/; LexisNexis, n.d., https://www.lexisnexis.com/en-us/gateway .page; Investopedia, n.d., https://www.investopedia.com/; Oxford English Dictionary, n.d., https://www.oed.com/; Merriam-Webster, n.d., https://www.merriam-webster.com.

95 Preqin, n.d., https://www.preqin.com/; PitchBook, n.d., https://pitchbook.com/; SEC.gov, n.d., https://www.sec.gov/; LexisNexis, n.d., https://www.lexisnexis.com/en-us/gateway .page; Investopedia, n.d., https://www.investopedia.com/; Oxford English Dictionary, n.d., https://www.oed.com/; Merriam-Webster, n.d., https://www.merriam-webster.com.

96 Barry P. Barbash and Jai Massari, "The Investment Advisers Act of 1940: Regulation by Accretion," Rutgers Law Journal 39.3 (2008).

97 Investment Advisers Act of 1940, 15 U.S.C. § 80b (2011).

98 Investment Advisers Act of 1940, 17 CFR § 275.203(l) (2011).

99 Investment Advisers Act of 1940, 15 U.S.C. § 80b(1)(2)(7) (2011).

100 Investment Advisers Act of 1940, 17 C.F.R. § 275.203(m)-1 (2011).

101 Investment Advisers Act of 1940, 15 U.S.C. § 80b-2(a)(11) (2011); Investment Advisers Act of 1940, 17 C.F.R. § 275.203A-1(b)(1)(B) (2011).

102 Investment Advisers Act of 1940, 15 U.S.C. § 80b (2011).

103 Investment Advisers Act of 1940, 17 C.F.R. § 275.205-3(c)(1)(B)(C) (2011).

104 Ahmad Takatkah, "VC Funds 101: Understanding Venture Fund Structures, Team Compensation, Fund Metrics and Reporting," Medium, VCpreneur, April 16, 2019, https://vcpreneur.com/vc-funds-101-understanding-venture-fund-structures-team -compensation-fund-metrics-and-reporting-152b02e8504a.

105 Preqin, n.d., https://www.preqin.com/; PitchBook, n.d., https://pitchbook.com/; SEC.gov, n.d., https://www.sec.gov/; LexisNexis, n.d., https://www.lexisnexis.com/en-us/gateway .page; Investopedia, n.d., https://www.investopedia.com/; Oxford English Dictionary, n.d., https://www.oed.com/; Merriam-Webster, n.d., https://www.merriam-webster.com.

106 Prohibitions relating to interstate commerce and the mails, 15 U.S.C. § 77 (2020).

107 Securities Act of 1933, 17 CFR § 230.501–506 (2021).

108 Investopedia, n.d., https://www.investopedia.com/.

109 SEC.gov, n.d., https://www.sec.gov/.

110 Securities Exchange Act of 1934, 17 CFR § 240.3a4-1 (2021).

111 Blackstreet Capital Management, LLC and Murry N. Gunty, SEC Administrative Proceeding, No. 3-17267 (June 1, 2016), https://www.sec.gov/litigation/admin/2016 /34-77959.pdf.

Contributor Bios

112 "Julie Castro Abrams — Gp — How Women Invest | Linkedin," n.d., https://www.linkedin .com/in/julie-castro-abrams.

113 "Our Team," Resolute Ventures, n.d., https://resolute.vc/team/.

114 "David Brown — Crunchbase Person Profile," Crunchbase, n.d., https://www.crunchbase .com/person/david-brown.

115 "John Burke — Managing Partner — Proof | Linkedin," n.d., https://www.linkedin.com/in /johnburke.

116 "About," Calixte Davis, n.d., https://www.calixtedavis.com/about.

117 "Josh Felser," Freestyle VC, February 7, 2022, https://freestyle.vc/team/josh-felser/.

118 "About," John Gannon Blog — Venture Capital Newsletter and VC Jobs, n.d., https://johngannonblog.com/about/.

119 "About," 1517 Fund, n.d., https://www.1517fund.com/.

120 "About," Grit Ventures, n.d., https://www.gritventures.com/team.

121 "Tracy Gray — Founder and Managing Partner — The 22 Fund | Linkedin," n.d., https://www.linkedin.com/in/tracydgray; "Home," Milken Institute, n.d., https://milkeninstitute.org/.

122 "Kirsten Green," Forerunner Ventures, n.d., https://www.forerunnerventures.com/team /kirsten-green.

123 "Charles Hudson," Precursor Ventures, n.d., https://precursorvc.com/team_member /charles-hudson/.

124 "Jim F. Jensen," Wilson Sonsini Goodrich & Rosati Professional Corporation Home Page — Palo Alto, Silicon Valley, San Francisco, New York, Seattle, San Diego, Washington, D.C., Shanghai, Hong Kong, Brussels — Jim F. Jensen, n.d., https://www.wsgr.com/en /people/jim-f-jensen.html.

125 "Eric Krichevsky — Founder/Owner — RYLNYC | Linkedin," n.d., https://www.linkedin .com/in/erickrichevsky.

126 Scott Kupor, "Scott Kupor," Andreessen Horowitz, n.d., https://a16z.com/author /scott-kupor/.

127 Frances Luu, personal interview.

128 "Team," LifeSci Venture Partners, n.d., https://www.lifesciventure.com/.

129 "Team," Township, n.d., https://township.agency/team.

130 "Alison Rosenthal," Stanford Graduate School of Business, n.d., https://www.gsb.stanford
     .edu/faculty-research/faculty/alison-rosenthal.

131 "Jason Rowley — Crunchbase Person Profile," Crunchbase, n.d., https://www.crunchbase
     .com/person/jason-donald-rowley.

132 "Expa Team," Expa, n.d., https://www.expa.com/team.

133 "People," Y Combinator, n.d., https://www.ycombinator.com/people/.

134 "About," 1517 Fund, n.d., https://www.1517fund.com/.

135 "Adam S. Tope: People: DLA Piper Global Law Firm," DLA Piper, n.d., https://www
     .dlapiper.com/en/us/people/t/tope-adam.

136 "Eric Woo, CFA — Revere VC Team," Revere VC | Team, n.d., https://www.reverevc.com
     /team/eric-woo-cfa.

137 "Team," Basis Set Ventures, n.d., https://www.basisset.com/team.

138 "Alan Yang — Principal and Director of Accounting Services — Towne Advisory Services
     Corp. | Linkedin," n.d., https://www.linkedin.com/in/alan-yang-8808a03.

139 Hustle Fund, n.d., https://www.hustlefund.vc/team.

140 "Timothy Young — President — Dropbox | Linkedin," n.d., https://www.linkedin.com/in
     /timhyoung.